commitment without ideology

commitment
without
ideology

THE EXPERIENCE OF CHRISTIAN GROWTH

BY
C. DANIEL BATSON
J. CHRISTIAAN BEKER
W. MALCOLM CLARK

A Pilgrim Press Book
from
United Church Press
Philadelphia

Library of Congress Cataloging in Publication Data

Batson, Charles Daniel, 1943–
  Commitment without ideology.

  "A Pilgrim Press book."
  Includes bibliographical references.
  1. Experience (Religion) I. Beker, Johan
Christiaan, 1924–   II. Clark, Warren Malcolm, 1936–
III. Title.
BV4916.B33   201'.1   72–13000
ISBN 0–8298–0245–2

The quotation on p. 5 is from *Sense and Nonsense* (Évanston, Ill.: Northwestern University Press, 1964), p. 96. Used by permission.

   The scripture quotations are (unless otherwise indicated) from the *Revised Standard Version of the Bible,* copyrighted 1946 and 1952 by the Division of Christian Education, National Council of Churches, and are used by permission. Biblical quotations marked NEB are from *The New English Bible, New Testament.* © The Delegates of the Oxford University Press and the Syndics of the Cambridge University Press 1961. Reprinted by permission.

United Church Press
1505 Race Street
Philadelphia, Pennsylvania 19102

At this point religion ceases to be a conceptual construct or an ideology and once more becomes part of the experience of interhuman life.

—*Maurice Merleau-Ponty*

acknowledgments

We would like to express special thanks to several people who greatly aided this project at certain stages. First, the seeds for many of our ideas lie in the work of James E. Loder. Our thinking has grown in a different direction from his, to the point that he would probably strongly disagree with the stance of this volume. But for some very fertile clues we happily give him thanks and hope that through further dialogue with him both our positions may be further enriched. Second, J. Randall Nichols participated in many of the discussions which led to the writing of this volume with a critical eye which has been most appreciated. A communications and homiletics expert, he has made the major contribution to a manuscript now in process which attempts a basic theoretical analysis of the implications of our proposed experiential theology for the practice of ministry. Indeed, much of his material would have been included in the present volume had space allowed.

Third, Roland W. Tapp served as an editorial consultant on the volume in its early stages, giving us both encouragement and assistance during that limbo of marketing the manuscript. Without his help you probably would not now have this book in your hands. Fourth, Nancy Stoup is to be thanked for her amazing speed and accuracy in typing much of the manuscript.

Finally, for continued support and patience throughout many long evenings of "the project" in Princeton, as well as daily during a vacation in Tennessee in the summer of 1971, our wives deserve special thanks. In many ways it is they who have borne the burden of our thought.

Princeton, New Jersey
C.D.B.
J.C.B.
W.M.C.

introduction

We propose a new understanding of what it means to be Christian based upon a new theological method. The title of this volume suggests the flavor of the new understanding; the subtitle the new theological method.

One of the few terms which remains an undisputedly relevant appellative for a Christian is "committed." A Christian is committed; he has faith. But such an observation quickly produces the question: To what is the Christian committed? Various answers to this question dot the history of Christianity: "To a belief in Jesus as the Son of God incarnate," "To the Apostles' Creed," "To the church," "To a Christian life-style." The list could be extended almost indefinitely. Some object to the way the question is phrased, asserting, "It's not to *what* but to *whom!*" They then offer their answer: "To Jesus Christ, the Lord of life," "To God active in Christ." Again, the list could grow long. Still others answer with ethical principles such as: "To love and serve one's fellowman."

Each of these answers seems to lead, albeit often unintentionally, to an ideology, to a conception of Christianity as a set of beliefs or principles describing true reality.[1] Indeed, commitment to something seems unavoidably to produce ideology. But is this bad? Must not the Christian, like anyone else, commit himself to something, especially in times of rapid change and uncertainty such as these? Is not one's task to pick carefully between ideologies?

Such a defense creates obvious problems in an age when the limitations of ideology have become woefully apparent. The dangers of ideologies, whether communist or capitalist, radical or conservative, Establishment or New Left, Consciousness II or III—the dangers of "the Movement" whatever the particular movement be—cry out from any newspaper or newscast. Ideologies stereotype and oversimplify. Ideologies prevent honest communication. Ideologies kill. And regrettably, Christian ideologies cannot plead innocence to such indictments any more than others, as the history of Christendom all too clearly documents.

In the claim to describe reality as it truly is or truly ought to be—the claim of any ideology—one inescapably develops a conceptual system which is unresponsive to new experiences. Rather than being shaped by experience as well as providing an interpretive context for making sense out of experience, an ideology becomes the standard of truth to which experience must conform. One's ideology, his most deeply held truth and concern, thus becomes his greatest oppressor. If then, as Christians, we come to the world with another ideology, even an ideology of freedom, love, peace, and forgiveness, we might best stay at home.

Is it possible, however, to speak of commitment without necessarily adopting an ideology? We believe it is. Our thesis is that not only does such a possibility exist but that the Christian gospel is open to precisely such commitment: commitment without ideology. The crucial aspect of such commitment is that it is not commitment to any*thing*. Each of the answers to the "Commitment to what?" question involves an object for Christian commitment, a "truth" which provides the key to reality. In contrast to this traditional approach, a focus upon the experience of faith itself suggests that *Christian commitment is not defined by its object—whether a doctrine, a person (either God or Jesus), or an ethical principle.* The Christian is not Christian because of what or even whom he has faith in.

Instead of being committed to some*thing, the Christian is challenged by Jesus to be committed to growth in a particular* *direction, outward toward others; and, moreover, to expression of this growth in responsible action.* The Christian is challenged by the life and teaching of Jesus to move away from his present stance and reality in the direction of increased exposure to and responsible interaction with his environment, without any clear specification of where such growth will lead.

This nonideological commitment in response to Jesus does not mean that there is no ideological content to the individual Christian's beliefs or that he lives without any view of reality. It does mean, however, that a Christian view of reality is unspecifiable in any general way, being totally contingent on a Christian's level of maturity and situation. The Christian is not called to live in ignorance of or isolation from ideologies and institutions, but to grow in the direction of an increased ability to reexamine continually the legitimacy of involvement with any given ideology or institution. Christians must work in and through such structures if they are to act responsibly in their environment, but they are challenged to resist capture by them. Christian growth is toward involvement in the social environment, but without the security blanket of a single ideology. A Christian's beliefs and consciousness, his reality, are continually changing.

If this proposed directional emphasis is correct, Christian experience need not involve particular beliefs (e.g., in God, in Christ, or in the resurrection) or a specific context (e.g., the institutional church). Indeed, the content and context of Christian experience may not be clearly "Christian" at all, being necessarily idiosyncratic to the particular individual in his social world. *It is the direction of growth which is Christian.* The content and context will not, of course, be unimportant to the individual, but they are not the critical characteristics of the experience. Critical is whether the experience functions to move him into increasingly responsible interaction with an increasingly large reality.

Such a thesis raises many questions. How does one grow in the direction of increased responsible involvement in one's social world and away from the insulating security of ideologies, whether Christian or non-Christian? What is the character of this growth experience? In what sense is it Christian? What is the role of the Bible in this process of Christian growth? Questions such as these have motivated our thought, discussion, and writing. These are not the questions which have usually motivated the theologian; he has more frequently been concerned to answer the referential questions of who or what God is, what the true nature of man may be, and how God and man relate. But in the search for a new approach to Christian theology, it is necessary not just to propose new answers to old questions. New questions themselves must be asked.

Pursuit of such questions has led us to seek a new method for doing theology, one which will not result in simply another Christian ideology. Accordingly, we are attempting to theologize from an experiential perspective. That is, rather than conceiving theology as a discipline concerned with consideration of the nature of God, man, and the relationship between them, as has been common in recent theology, theology is here conceived as an attempt to understand or make sense of *lived Christian experience.* The former approach has tended, albeit unwittingly, to lead to an enslaving morass of metaphysical assertions and problems, for it is basically an ideological attempt to describe true reality. A grand redemptive drama is played out on a cosmological stage, the plot being built around such concepts as *imago Dei,* the fall, original sin, incarnation, resurrection, grace, justification, the triune God, or the "new man in Christ." Such theologies pit their Christian ideology against those of communism, secularism, scientism, etc.

In contrast, our experiential theology seeks to make sense of the Christian experience as lived both in antiquity and today. In so doing it challenges the importance of this redemptive drama and the related concepts, suggesting that the attempt to describe a Christian reality which they imply is not the central concern of the Christian gospel. Rather, the language of the gospel is an attempt to express a lived experience. If theology is to offer more than a Christian ideology, it must be grounded in the gospel as lived and spoken. *Theology must be derivative from the religious life and language, not determinative of it.* Theological concepts grow out of an attempt to make sense of the Christian language, which has in turn emerged from attempts to express and evoke an experience of Christian growth.

While far from unimportant, theological concepts are thus a step removed from the dynamic regenerative thrust of the Christian gospel. The concern of the proposed experiential theology is to probe back through Christian language to the experience which lies behind it, allowing an examination of the functional dynamics of that experience, including what happens within the individual and how it affects his living. Only through such a process does it seem possible to tune one's theological concepts to the experience they are developed to help understand.

But how is one to go about doing theology experientially? A major insight of existential phenomenology, to be outlined in chapter 2, forms the cornerstone of the present attempt. *The so-called "real" world of things and persons is actually the product of human linguistic and conceptual construction on unreflected or "primordial" lived experience.* Any ideology, Christian or otherwise, assumes that one's conceptual system describes things as they truly are or ought to be. Operating within a phenomenological framework, we shall attempt to examine primordial Christian experience and the "real" linguistic and conceptual world it has produced, always recognizing the latter as relative, not absolute. So conceived, Christian language and theological concepts are seen as modes of expression of a primordial experience, not as descriptions of a metaphysical or ontological reality.[2] The language is not changed, but the assumptions as to how it functions are.

An experiential theology is not a totally unique idea. The present approach has classic parallels in the history of doctrine. Considering the broader sweep of the history of Christian theology, the two major foci of the proposed experiential theology—Christian experience and, closely related, Christian growth—have classic antecedents which must be noted briefly. The insistence that Christian theology focus upon the experience of the man of faith received its most famous expression in the work of Friedrich Schleiermacher. He conceived theology to be a description of religious self-consciousness characterized by a feeling of absolute dependence, which presupposes the existence of God. Although we are following Schleiermacher in the concern of experience, we oppose his particular approach.

For he still seems to focus upon a description of true reality. In *The Christian Faith,* he seeks to describe the true nature of Christian experience and on the basis of this analysis to describe both the character of the world and divine attributes. In contrast, we seek to understand the dynamic process and function of Christian experience as lived, not to describe its necessary character in terms of content.

The second major theme of the proposed experiential theology is a developmental emphasis, a focus upon the process of Christian growth. As John Hick suggests in *Evil and the God of Love,* one can characterize the development of Western theology by two general theological types: the dominant Augustinian approach, which emphasizes man's fallenness due to misused freedom, and the Irenaean approach. The latter emphasizes the process of Christian growth and development in God's continuing providence, culminating in the final "likeness" of God. Clearly, the present theology falls in the Irenaean rather than the Augustinian camp, for it emphasizes the process of Christian growth and finds a doctrinal treatment of man's fall largely irrelevant. It resides with Irenaeus uneasily, however, attempting to approach the experience of Christian growth not through specification of a teleological goal toward which one aspires (the likeness of God) but through change in a particular direction, that of responsible involvement in one's social world. Thus, although there are definite affinities between the present approach and those of Schleiermacher and Irenaeus, there are major differences. To a large degree these differences stem from our radically different philosophical assumptions. Western theology has tended to employ either an idealist or realist philosophical base. Existential phenomenology is an attempt to walk a tightrope between these two classic alternatives, opposing each. Experiential theology has accompanied Christian dogmatics through the centuries, mostly as a protest against the danger of overintellectualism, dogmatic rigidity, and finesse.

Whenever and wherever the focus has been on the sanctification of the believer, on manifestations of the Holy Spirit, or on conversion, experiential theology has erupted on the scene. From the days of Irenaeus, Christian history is dotted with experiential approaches: one recalls the moral influence theory of Abélard and the fourteenth century's pervasive streams in the Medieval Mystic Tradition; the Brothers of the Common Life— Geert Grote, the "Imitatio Christi" of Thomas à Kempis; movements within the Left-wing Reformation, especially Menno Simons' reformulation of the Baptist anarchic revolutionary tradition; later, since the seventeenth century, the Pietist movements on the Continent and in America; Spener in Germany; the Réveil in Holland, Switzerland, and France, men like Alexandre Vinet, and in the United States, the several Revival movements such as that of Jonathan Edwards. One also recalls the Wesley brothers and Methodism on the frontier; still later the brothers Blumhardt in Bethel, Germany; not to mention the great Christian hymn writers, Aquinas, Luther, Gerhard, Tersteegen; all of this climaxing in Schleiermacher's *The Christian Faith*.

The resurgence of the Jesus movement in our day makes it imperative to reconsider the scope of a responsible experiential theology, so that common sense and sober reflection be not buried under a stream of ecstatic behavior.

Now a few remarks on recent parallels to our experiential theology. In the last few years several attempts to theologize from a phenomenological base have been explored. Sociologist Peter Berger's *A Rumor of Angels* is largely theological, and some recent writings of Dietrich Ritschl and Paul Ricoeur are in the direction of a phenomenologically based theology. While not explicitly phenomenological, Bernard Lonergan's *Insight* moves along a parallel track in analyzing the expansiveness of one's knowledge of reality. Certainly the best developed explicit attempt at using phenomenology as a base for Christian theology is Langdon Gilkey's *Naming the Whirlwind: The Renewal of God-Language*. Although we have found his thought most helpful and encouraging, we feel that Gilkey has not fully capitalized upon the potential of phenomenology, largely owing to the particular interpretations of transcendence and metaphysics he employs. Gilkey tends to rely upon German phenomenology for his orientation. In contrast, we have relied more heavily on the treatment of transcendence and metaphysics in the late writings of the French existential phenomenologist Maurice Merleau-Ponty, especially his posthumous

The Visible and the Invisible. The resulting differences on these key concepts produce a striking divergence between the present work and Gilkey's, both in the questions asked and in suggested answers.

Also, as many readers will no doubt recognize, there are some affinities in the concerns expressed here and those of the recent "death of God" theology. Yet there are also clear differences. With "death of God" theologians such as William Hamilton and Paul van Buren we share deep concern over the sad state of the current theological enterprise, especially the tendency toward abstract conceptuality not grounded in the life of man. Yet we take strong issue with, for example, Van Buren's attempt to translate God statements into man statements. The way to deal with our present theological crisis is not through a "reduction" or "secularization" of the gospel but through a reconsideration of the relationship of one's theological concepts to the religious experience they were developed to interpret.

A recent attempt to theologize by focusing upon the experience of Christian faith deserves special mention: Richard R. Niebuhr's *Experiential Religion.* His work parallels ours in many ways. Niebuhr both makes use of a phenomenological approach and attempts to respond to the culture gap between the world of the Bible and that of contemporary man without compromising the integrity of either. There are two major divergences between his focus and ours, however. First, while we consider the experience of Christian faith to concern new meaning, the transformation of one's reality, and thereby new action, Niebuhr considers the focus to involve one's response to power. Second, following the pattern of many phenomenological analyses, Niebuhr seeks to describe the affective states which form the content of the experience of faith. In contrast, we follow the more functional emphasis of the derivatives of phenomenology in Gestalt psychology, focusing upon the dynamic process of Christian growth. Rather than considering *what* psychic states are involved in the experience of Christian growth, we have sought to uncover *how* the growth process occurs, both within the individual and the community. This dynamic emphasis produces a concern for functional explanations relative to the descriptive cataloging of the content of a particular experience.

But in analyzing the content of Christian experience, Niebuhr's descriptive work is an extremely valuable supplement to our own. Indeed, it complements the present study so well that a reader might be advised to consider it a helpful companion volume.

A few comments should be made about the structure of this book. If the reader's experience parallels ours, he is skeptical as soon as he picks up a volume with multiple authorship. Is it simply scraps pasted together at random? Is it many people saying the same thing again and again? Is it a collection of superficial overviews of various aspects of a problem without engaging major issues? We have attempted to keep such questions in mind throughout the discussions which produced this book in hopes of preventing it from being any of these. And positively, we think we have several points on our side. First, though obviously interested in theology, no one of us is first and foremost a theologian in the classic sense. This has, we think, allowed us to come to our task with a fresher view than might have been possible otherwise. Second, each of us occupies a different disciplinary niche. Together we combine a range of interests including Old and New Testament studies, biblical theology, linguistics, philosophy, psychology, and religious education. This range has enabled us to address a broader range of issues than any one of us could alone. Such breadth seems essential in attempting to explore the potential of a new theological approach, especially one which focuses on experience and therefore must draw from many disciplines other than traditional theology. Third, this book has emerged from a long series of conversations among the authors. Because of this it has been possible to develop a unified argument from chapter to chapter.

In Part One a number of questions are raised which anyone doing Christian theology today must face. Part Two outlines our approach to a response to these questions through experiential theology. To this end, chapter 2 presents the basic thrust and assumptions of the new approach, setting it in the context of recent theological motifs; chapter 3 focuses upon an analysis of the psychodynamics of Christian experience and the relation of Christian experience and language. Part Three examines the biblical basis and implications of the proposed experiential theology. Chapters 4 and 5 focus upon the Old Testament. Through numerous concrete illustrations chapter 4 examines the character of religious experience expressed in the Old Testament and the interaction of this experience with its linguistic forms. Chapter 5 considers the social and cultural context of Israel which led to its form of religious experience and expression, unique in the ancient Near East. Chapter 6 turns to the New Testament and speaks to the specifically hermeneutical implications of our approach, proposing a "hermeneutic of experience" and employing this hermeneutic in a test case analysis of Paul's use of resurrection. Part Four contains a summary chapter which brings together the threads of argument.

Finally, a word of caution may be in order. Although we will be critical of much theology, we too are attempting to theologize—from Christian experience. But our intent is not to present you with experience per se, either of our own or others. Indeed, we have tended to avoid any specific examples or illustrations of Christian experience. Examples, though they may aid conceptual understanding, are, seemingly, too understandable; they tend to generate a conceptual closure alien to our present concern. But it is also true that some experience seems essential if what we are saying is to resonate at all. From whence should this experience come? We think it must come from the reader. Only as he brings with him his own experience—experience which he would in some sense call religious, if not Christian—only to this degree will what follows be more than an empty conceptual thesis. And, quite likely, only to this degree will many of the correctives our argument needs emerge.

part one

The
Theological
Heritage

the function of the
bible today

J. CHRISTIAAN BEKER

Anyone who dares to do Christian theology today, who seeks to express the value of the Bible for modern man, is first and foremost faced with an onslaught of questions. The basic question is: Can any theology do the job of revitalizing the Bible? And in the discussion around the Bible, is the alternative correct: biblical history or biblical kerygmatic theology? Are we, caught in this alternative, not responsible for the rejection of biblical studies today—for avoiding the heart of the Bible, viz., the consideration of the relevance of biblical religion for us today? Does an experiential approach carry any hope for a new way of doing theology more responsibly? The chapters which follow suggest an affirmative answer to this question. But first some questions facing any attempt at a biblically based theology must be confronted.[1]

I
THE ALTERNATIVE:
"HISTORY OR THEOLOGY"

The hope for a vital rebirth of the Bible has for years been invested in the biblical theologian. The biblical theologian would overcome, it was expected, the historicism and rationalism of biblical research and allow the biblical revelation to come alive for our contemporary situation. This hope has now collapsed. The collapse is evident in the crisis around the Bible in our seminaries and universities. In these institutions the questions appear most sharply. The "strange new world" of the Bible has become so strange to the average student that he no longer can find the bridge between his world of meaning and the biblical world. The alienation of the Bible is the predominant issue in theology today. This observation is commonplace and deserves our interest, mainly because it does not occur at the end of a period of biblical historicism and unconcern with the theological elements of the Bible but, rather, precisely at the end of a period of a most active theological and hermeneutical biblical concern. Biblical theology seems to have given birth to the crisis of the biblical field. This ironic statement merits reflection.

It is clear that neo-orthodoxy sponsored the interest in biblical theology and that with the apparent collapse of systematic theology, and neo-orthodoxy in particular, biblical theology itself collapsed. Too little did we notice in the past how biblical theology came to depend on the vigor of dogmatic theology, so much so that, for instance, Karl Barth's systematic theology was simply called biblical theology. Too little did we heed the voices of the originators of biblical theology both in Pietism and in the Enlightenment, who conceived of biblical theology precisely as a defense against the inroads of systematic theology. A position of defense, however, never yields a positive definition. Thus, throughout its history the definition of biblical theology has swung back and forth between its characterization as a historical-descriptive discipline (Gabler-Wrede-Stendahl) and as a theological discipline as well (Hofmann-Bultmann-Ebeling). This dilemma of biblical theology has found expression in the perennial debate about history versus faith, *Historie versus Geschichte;* and the alternative history *or* kerygma constituted the field of the debate.

It seems to me that this alternative, in the form "biblical history or biblical theology," is a dead issue. The basic question today is: With what perspective do we approach the Bible? And in the discussion around the Bible, is the alternative correct: biblical history or biblical kerygmatic theology? Are we, caught in this alternative, not responsible for the rejection of biblical studies today—for avoiding the heart of the Bible, namely, the consideration of the relevance of biblical religion for us today? Let me illustrate concretely the sterility of the present alternative: history or theology. I will first present the case against theology, since it has always claimed "relevancy," over against the so-called irrelevance of purely historical scholarship, and since its present collapse, notwithstanding its urge toward relevance, is so ironical.

The Case Against Theology
For too long biblical vitality has been associated with biblical theology. In too many faculty discussions the sure way to relieve the crisis around the Bible and to make the Bible come alive is to attach biblical courses to theological courses, so that it can be demonstrated that biblical conceptuality informs our present thinking about issues. This praiseworthy effort obscures the fact that the so-called biblical conceptuality is, in fact, often a formulation by systematic theology—not so much exegetically derived from scripture but read into and placed onto scripture via certain abstractions such as "kerygma," "God's act in history," "eschatological act of salvation." What is more serious, however, is that, in such combination courses with theological subject matter, the biblical theologian tends to jump away from the text to the present situation—so that the biblical experience is ignored in its living context and, thus isolated, receives whatever modern appeal it can carry. Too often, theologians' interpretations of texts are simply fanciful meditations on modern problems with an occasional paraphrase of and reference to biblical material. The student then is not led to the Bible but, rather, away from the Bible, and so concentrates—albeit armed with a biblical concept—not on the biblical religious environment but on some modern problem.

The vital error, however, is that biblical vitality is here confused with a theological conceptuality. Thus, a student is led to believe that once he has grasped a biblical "category" the Bible itself can be dispensed with. And so the biblical theologian has enriched the "sloganitis" of theology: Terms like "kerygma," "eschatology," "the Word," "God's act in Christ," have lost nearly all precise exegetical meaning. However, not only has precise exegetical meaning been lost but *meaning* as such. The crisis of biblical theology is exactly the crisis of *the condensed category* which has lost its symbolic value and thus becomes a verbal abstraction. The biblical theologian under neo-orthodox aegis has been caught in playing the game of "theological categories"; and since neo-orthodoxy built its case against Schleiermacher, realities like experience and the religious man were condemned as perversions of the unique revelatory acts of God and his word. So the biblical theologian confused biblical revelation with a conceptuality of it in ontological categories. The much-hallowed "word of God," which like a true *dabar* creates its own dynamic meaning in the hearer, has become too often a hollow phrase because its experiential referent was taken for granted. Now, however, the very meaningfulness of those "self-evident" categories is at stake, and because the categories lack experiential verification, the whole enterprise of biblical theology itself is at stake. Clarity on this point necessitates a careful distinction between religious-symbolic and theological-interpretative language.

There is an enormous credibility gap in our time between the theological category and our own life-style, with the result that the theological category meets with increasing indifference. The divorce between category and experience—and the neglect of this issue by the biblical theologian for the sake of the "infinite difference" between biblical revelation and human religiosity—is the direct reason for the collapse of biblical theology. For many of us biblical theology has become a juggling of concepts and a word game in a world which has no contact with ours. The rebirth of *biblical theology* depends on its willingness to contemplate the possibility of a return to *biblical religion*.

The Case Against History

Whereas biblical theology tends to jump away from the biblical text to the modern situation with the conceptual abstraction, biblical criticism and history tend to move away from the text to the hinterland of archaeology and to the particulars of the historical past. Whereas biblical theology short-circuits the hermeneutical task by means of the theological abstraction and unconcern with exegetical precision and context, biblical history shows no concern for the hermeneutical task at all. Thus students correctly complain that the modernizing of biblical theology is matched by the archaizing of biblical history.

What this means to the student is obvious. Whereas the theological curriculum gives a special place to the biblical department, since the Bible is supposedly the source of all Christian truth and the provider of essential religious equipment, the student now wonders why he is not studying the Bible in the department of history as a purely historical document. He therefore has no reason to ask existential questions and finds himself again in an utterly strange world alienated from his own. What makes the alienation so difficult to bear is not the historical study of an ancient document in itself, for such is the case in the study of all ancient texts and all historical investigation, but the tacit presupposition that the Bible is of course a highly meaningful book to him. The alienation is painful because of the contradiction between implication and actuality. This general problem is worsened by our classical exegetical practice. The average student becomes the information can, filled with a bewildering variety of historical details and particulars but usually not assisted to understand the particulars in terms of the whole. Biblical historical criticism, especially because of its literary, form-critical interests, has brought about an atomizing of history which kills a sense of totality. In other words, the student's historical imagination is not kindled, and his knowledge and understanding of ancient cultures is usually exceedingly poor. The amazing lack of interest in and knowledge of ancient history is well known. Thus, the opportunity of stirring the historical imagination and of stirring an indirect hermeneutical interest is lost. The biblical scholar, in his care for detail and for the complexity of particulars, too often lacks the vision of the cultural outlook as a whole. Yet it is only in terms of the whole that an exegesis of particular texts makes sense. The sociology of knowledge, for instance, could give the biblical historian the opportunity to show the variety of world views and ideologies in terms of which biblical periods must be understood and in terms of which our own must be viewed.

However this may be, it is clear that our historical exegesis and criticism is in trouble because it presents to the student an outdated encyclopedia, no longer consulted because it fails to make contact with the issues of his own life. The conclusion seems unmistakable: The present understanding of the alternative "history or theology" is no longer an option for us as a way back to the vitality of the Bible.

II
THE PRESENT
SITUATION

When we speak about our age as a "secular" age, we refer to a reality which defies precise definition but which manifests itself in a bewildering variety of ways. We hear how modern man is dominated by contingency, temporality, relativity, and a sense of autonomy. What seems central is the feeling that the logos—a principle of order, stability, and meaning—has dropped out of life. The breakdown of a dominant metaphysical system has created a sense of uncertainty and flux. There is no longer a central symbolic system in terms of which the individual can order his values and life. There seems to be no objectivity about anything in "outer" reality, so that no "outer-directedness" is possible as a way of finding oneself in the right. The behavioral sciences have taught us the amazing contingencies of our lives; the sociological and psychological determinants of our lives rob us of any sense of permanence and ultimate meaning. What people deemed to be eternal verities and meanings have proved to be dubious ideologies, if not idolatries. The pluralism in our society is overwhelming, and an increasing variety of reality definitions has come about. The cultural pluralism contains both a promise and a threat: a promise because the monopoly of an established ideology is much more vulnerable, which in turn allows freer recourse to felt experience; a threat because man is tempted to seek his security in technological success and will then be reduced to a machine. The scientific orientation has created a one-dimensional man, the man with the horizontal view who increasingly knows himself to be the master of his fate and who views life as a conquest toward his own comfort and success.

What does this atmosphere mean for the man of faith?

A. He is confronted with the question which Albert Camus

has stated for our age with unusual clarity and sharpness: Is religious faith a denial of being a human being? Is faith in God an essential part of being responsibly human, or is it surrender of being human, that is, a cop-out, an escapist resolution or safety clause for someone not daring to face an absurd world without a deus ex machina—God as problem solver? Is man a haphazard accident in biological evolution or is he a creature of God? And if the latter, how does a genuine religious outlook operate? What is its function and how is it possible?

B. Thus confronted, the man of faith must observe the breakdown of the theological and ecclesiological tradition. And this tradition is suspect to him, not only because divine truth is claimed for exceedingly contingent statements, not only because the relativism of everything historical corrodes the dogmatic traditions and confessions of the church, but especially because the alliance between establishment and church in the past has betrayed the revolutionary impulses of the gospel. The question is: How will he face the ritual of the community in which he was born and manage to make an honest decision in terms of which he can distinguish between the belief system of the church and the faith he can honestly stand for?

C. Amid the cultural and theological confusion there is an urge toward simplicity and intellectual honesty, toward the differentiation between having and being, between having all the intellectual information or cultural goods and being a genuine person, not claiming to "own" more than one can carry. There is an urge in our confusion toward "traveling light": to walk with what is absolutely necessary rather than be burdened with superfluous externals. Thus the breakdown of self-evident structures in our culture can become an opportunity toward a new clarity of what one can honestly own—of a new life-style based on a stance rooted in our own experience and not something simply borrowed from extraneous sources. Too many people accept the end product of Christian theology, that is, the system of interpretations given by others to their understanding of the Christian faith and thus the dogmatic overlay of Christianity. We then equate the dogmatic interpretation of others with revelation itself and so become borrowers and parasites, equating a religious stance with a conceptual system, looking everywhere but in ourselves for the truth of what we ourselves can affirm. Why is seminary education so often characterized as a "head trip?" Why is the minister so often no longer a charismatic leader but a second-rate sociologist? How long can a man live off the religious experiences of others and claim them as his own?

D. If the category of *experience* is of new importance today, it is equally clear that the theological scene witnesses the alienation of the theological *concept*. The sterility of theology is exactly this: It takes the biblical experience for granted and does not clearly investigate the relation of experience and word. The biblical-theological concept has lost its symbolic character; it has become language without grounding in felt experience. The word has ceased to be a symbol and has become a sign pointing to a world which has lost contact with the world of meaning we inhabit. And thus the biblical concept has become ossified or frozen language, carrying on a pseudo-existence of its own. It now operates as an ontological, reified category which *dictates to* my experience rather than *derives from* my experience. The exploration of the relation between experience and its conceptual expression is made so difficult in the Christian tradition because of its strong theological, doctrinal inheritance. The norm of being a Christian has always rested in the confessional statement, and the claim of orthodoxy over against heresy usually rests in assent to doctrinal propositions. Therefore the relation between concept and experience is usually reversed. One does not travel the road from experience to the concept as its expression. Rather, one gives assent to an intellectual abstraction which is subsequently inflated with religious sentiment. Thus, confusion reigns and the conflict between necessary beliefs and authentic faith is created.

My point is that there is an enormous credibility gap in our time between the theological categories and our own life-style, with the result that the theological category, however biblical in origin, meets with increasing indifference. Thus the return to biblical religion seems mandatory, just as the authority of the Bible does not lie in a new formulation of its canonicity but in a trust that the biblical text itself will engender its own authority in touching the questions of my life. Unless we want to foster a wholesale return to every type of mysticism and drug experimentation, the biblical theologian should be occupied with a recovery of biblical religion, i.e., with the development of a responsible hermeneutic. He should break out of the false alternative of history or theology and should learn again what is involved in a religious stance—a religious perception of reality; in other words, he should turn to the primordial religious questions and perceptions and see how they are nourished, corrected, or judged by the religious experience of the biblical writers.

The man of faith today wants to know in a secular age and a one-dimensional technological world what it means to be religious, how revelation functions in the ordinary life situation, and how a religious perception of reality is possible. This new quest for transcendence, for possibilities of new meaning, and for a new perspective of his world cannot be stilled by the theological category and the packaged theological definition, or by a predetermined definition of reality—but it can possibly be stilled by guiding him to the "strange new world" of the Bible as the witness of religious men who have attained wholeness in such a religious stance as part and parcel of their concrete humanity. The real task of the theologian today is a preoccupation with the question of a return to biblical religion—the question of how the biblical texts *function* religiously. The crucial question is: Is the biblical text able to engender religious perception or not? Can the biblical text speak creatively to our present religious conflicts? If not, then there is no reason for a return to the Bible except as a historical document behind the cultural phenomenon of Christendom. The overcondemned *homo religiosus* of neo-orthodoxy—equated with idolatry and pharisaism—is clearly the answer to the longing of our time. The theological celebration of the secular man as the man "come of age" and as the technocrat royally ruling over a desacralized creation has justly come to an end, and will hopefully not be replaced by a new sacred or Christian world view, a new ideology.

THE PROBLEM
OF A RETURN
TO BIBLICAL RELIGION

A

The return to biblical religion should not be understood simply as a return to a biblicism and pietism which equates the Bible with the Word of God and resists historical-critical methodology. The *viva vox evangelii* is not to be confused with a bibliolatry, and the vitality of the Bible is not to be guaranteed in advance by a doctrine of the Word of God and revelation. The Reformation call to a return to the Bible as the sole source of Christian truth must in our day be heard in a radically different sense, without dogmatic and allegorical trappings. Yet it should be heard over against a dogmatic tradition which has encapsulated biblical truth with its own dogmatic theological weight and has regarded the Bible too often as a historical source legitimizing a dogmatic tradition rather than a religious source which enables religious perception to be born ever anew.

A simplified return to biblical religion is impossible because the split "biblical religion over against dogmatic tradition" is wrong. A modern modification of a return to scripture must face a radical problem, namely, that the Bible itself is an integral part of the tradition and that it is a library of documents of considerable literary, religious, and theological variety. The Bible cannot be divorced from the dogmatic tradition of the church, since it is itself the earliest part of that tradition. The point is: The Bible itself is in many ways a theological document and not simply a religious document. There are varieties of theologies in the Bible, theological and traditional interpretations of an original religious perception which no longer convey the birth of the religious perception. The mixture of religious perception and its theological interpretation causes the problem, especially since the conceptual interpretation tends to suffocate the religious experience which originally engendered it. The theological interpretation then becomes an extraneous, dogmatic authority, since modern man has no idea within himself of how the interpretation was arrived at. The problem becomes increasingly serious when in the course of time the theological conceptuality is transmitted, whereas its experiential base is forgotten. Historical and cultural distance thus aggravates the divorce between concept and experience. And so the increasing divorce between the religious perception and its interpretation is the reason for increasing mistrust and "irrelevance" of biblical assertions, the more so because the biblical theologian fastens himself to the variety of theological interpretations and categories—to the biblical conceptuality—rather than to the coming into being of the originating revelatory moment. In this context, neo-orthodoxy's appeal to Paul's theological conceptuality and its neglect of "Jesus" material in the Gospels should be noted.

The return to biblical religion then is conditioned by the solution of this dilemma. And the key question is: Will it be possible to uncover the road by which the religious perception became related to the interpretation of it? In other words, will it be possible to recover the meaning of the theological concept as the symbol which orders and gives expression to the religious perception? What is the exact relation between faith and the belief system? If the theological concept is to be an adequate, meaningful deposit of the faith perspective, then it must be made intelligible how such theological expression came into being from the faith perspective. It is meaningless, for instance, for me to accept the salvation concepts about Jesus Christ as to his miraculous birth, death, and resurrection unless it is clear to me how man's experience with Jesus occasioned such interpretations. For from what perspective can a set of theological concepts be meaningfully related to my world of experience when these concepts come to me from a source outside of me and are extraneous and alien to my world? In that case I accept the conviction of *others* as revelatory for *myself* without basic substantiation. Apostolic authority then becomes the locus of revelation rather than God's own revelatory authority over me.

The relation between experience and conceptuality or interpretation, then, is a key issue for hermeneutics. The more the conceptuality is divorced from the experience, the less religious meaning it carries. This problem is probably more serious for the New Testament than for the Old Testament, since the relation between experience and its expression can more easily be traced in the Old Testament and since its conceptual apparatus is less speculative and abstract, more concerned with historical, earthy concreteness than with apocalyptic and Gnostic speculations about a supranatural world. For it is exactly the supranaturalist framework of the New Testament which in our a-metaphysical age has become so problematic. Now the science of hermeneutics has always recognized the problem which I posit as the problem of an abiding experience within changing categories. Thus, the hermeneutical problem has traditionally been stated in some such form as this: Is there any continuity of experience in a world of radical change? Is there any continuity between the biblical world view and ours? It is the problem to which Karl Barth addressed himself by pointing to *die Sache* (subject matter) which remains the same, notwithstanding the variety of its linguistic expressions; it is the attempt of Rudolf Bultmann's demythologizing, which locates the continuity in the kerygma that confronts man's self-understanding; it is the various ways in which biblical theologians have distinguished between *Sprachgestalt* (language form) and *Sachverhalt* (material content); in other words, it is the complex problem of the interaction between faith and history.

My complaint, however, is that the problem has not been stated in terms of the relation between experience and its conceptuality. Thus the hermeneutical problem has been posited in an intellectualized fashion as *die Sache, the* kerygma, *the* word, in terms of a conceptuality, the experiential referent of which is exactly at stake! If such a concept has no meaning to my world of experience, "God's act in Christ" is no more a continuous reality between the New Testament world and my world than Gnostic or apocalyptic speculations. The question is rather: In terms of what experience is such a conceptual formulation meaningful? How can we bridge the relation between the originating experience and the conceptuality in which it is expressed? Is there the possibility of an abiding experience, notwithstanding the divergence of world views, which provides the various conceptual expressions of the experience?

The problem is complicated because we cannot simply posit an abiding continuing experience amid the discontinuity of world views. We cannot in any naïve manner separate the husk from the core, separate the particular conceptuality of a world view from the experience which lies behind it, and then claim that this experience has an abiding continuity with our world of experience. At this point an ontology of revelation provides an easier solution, since it posits a revelatory "substance" as the continuum within the discontinuity of world views. The argument from experience, however, distrusts such an ontological argument, since it is precisely the meaning of the ontological revelation which is at stake.

What must be clarified are two issues: (1) The characteristic differences between the biblical *world view* and our *own*, so that it becomes clear how a particular age thinks and how that thinking uses a conceptuality and an intellectual apparatus which is no longer ours. (2) The complex interaction between *world view* and *experience*. In order to avoid a simple solution to the problem of an abiding experience and changing categories, it cannot be posited that once we travel the road from the New Testament concept to the experience behind it we can appropriate the experience and merely dress it in a different, namely, modern, conceptuality. The problem is exactly the determination of the abiding element in the experience. This is such a difficult problem because world view, conceptuality, and experience interact and determine each other profoundly. This interaction between experience and world view, experience and conceptuality, is indeed the great relativizer. It is the decisive factor in the indifference of so many people toward the New Testament as a meaningless book for our age. For not only is the New Testament's conceptuality alien to our world but the bulk of the experience which produced the conceptuality is alien to us as well.

Rudolf Bultmann's recognition of this problem led him to demythologizing as a hermeneutic of existential interpretation. Yet the question remains whether he has done justice to the actual experience of biblical man; whether he has not "modernized" that experience too quickly because of a philosophical definition of myth which concentrates more on the elimination of myth than on the world of mythical experience. The continuity between the biblical world and ours is asserted in terms of the twin categories of self-understanding and the kerygma or word of God. However, it is exactly the lack of the experiential referent which makes kerygma, word of God, and decision of faith abstract ontological categories to us, however existentially presented.

A particular world view engenders experiences which are no longer meaningful or experiential for a different world view. A person inhabiting a mythical world view of which angels and demons are an integral part has no difficulty experiencing the reality of such angelic beings. A similar observation is to be made with respect to the resurrection experiences of the apostles. The denial of the reality of these experiences would constitute the insertion of a modern world view into an ancient apocalyptic world view and would thus be inappropriate. The point is simply that world view and experience interact; that the reality of an apocalyptic world view made possible resurrection experiences for the apostles which can no longer be accommodated by people who reject the apocalyptic world view.

However complex the interaction is between world view and personal experience, the abiding element must be sought very pragmatically in those experiences which have a meaningful relation to our world of experience. It would seem arrogant to make absolute judgments here about true and false: I can never judge the ultimate validity of someone's experience—I do not possess ontological criteria for doing so—I can only evaluate its meaningfulness or meaninglessness in terms of my own world of experience. In this way I do not make *my* world view the absolute criterion for truth, something Bultmann tends to do. Fully recognizing the particularity and tentativeness of my own world view, I can evaluate experiences of people in other times and places only in terms of their relation to my actual world of experience. The "real," then, is located in an honest assessment of what I can truly own, of what can honestly be made an integral part of my experience. For my world of experience should never be rigidly defined in advance. It is of the nature of experience to be open to the new, yet in such a manner that it is an integral part of my growth as a person and not an artificial parasitic growth, which disintegrates rather than integrates my personhood.

The problem of a return to biblical religion becomes critical when the bridge between experience and world view can no longer be found; when the divorce between the experience and concept has become so great that the concept takes on a life of its own, becomes frozen, objectified, and literalized, and is taken for granted as the way things are. The conceptual system thus becomes an ideology, a means of indoctrination, which however internalized has no longer a referent to felt experience. When this happens, religious statements become vacuous doctrinal propositions.

A return to biblical religion is possible, then, only when I can (1) trace the relation between the revelatory experience and its conceptuality, (2) honestly assess what kinds of biblical experience have a possible correlation to my world of experience, and (3) refrain from ontological statements and categories as prejudging the limits of my world of experience and as dictating in advance "the way it is."

It would seem that in this respect both the sociology of knowledge and phenomenology are crucial tools for the Christian theologian. Whereas the sociology of knowledge makes possible an imaginative hermeneutic of the various world views and ideologies, phenomenology in resisting ontological statements can help us to delineate and clarify the nature of experience and its relation to symbols. The problems surrounding a new hermeneutical approach will be discussed more adequately in chapter 6. The search for an "abiding experience," it will be suggested, is misleading, because a hermeneutic of experience cannot hope to distill a package of experience—an abiding content—out of the Bible and insert it into our experience. Besides, "abiding experience" suggests not only a transmissable *content* of experience but also a naïve conception of the relation of language to experience, as if experience were only incidentally and casually related to language.

B

The problem of a return to biblical *religion* as opening up for modern man the possibility of a religious life-style is especially acute for the New Testament. For the predominant framework in which *religious experience* is couched in the New Testament is the apocalyptic world view and *conceptuality.* And the collision between the apocalyptic world view and the modern world view is so pronounced that for modern man the apocalyptic world view does not establish any contact with the world of his felt experience. If anywhere, the alienation between concept and experience is striking here. The result is that apocalyptic conceptuality operates as a vacuous abstraction or a meaningless theological proposition.

Within the confines of this essay I cannot give a phenomenology of the apocalyptic world view and thus cannot describe the feelings and thinking of the man who inhabits the apocalyptic world. It is therefore not my intention to discuss the difficult problem of the experiential level which is inherent in the apocalyptic world view, the extent to which, within apocalypticism itself, a divorce is taking place between conceptualization and experiential meaning. There can be no doubt, however, that men like the apostles were apocalypticists who, contrary to Bultmann, were not demythologizers, but for whom apocalyptic realities were part of their experience.

My concern is a hermeneutical concern, namely, how modern man with his secular mentality can possibly relate to an apocalyptic world view, how his world of experience can possibly be hooked up with the apocalyptic experience and conceptuality of the New Testament. Such a hookup seems nearly impossible, especially since apocalypticism is schematized and objectified eschatology. In apocalypticism, images of hope have become frozen into an ontological reality which as the heavenly world of God is already prepared in supernature and merely awaits the time for its predetermined descent on earth, where it will abolish history and this world and establish the divine new age.

Apocalypticism then is the bridge between prophecy and speculative theology; it is the bridge which propels thought away from living experience to supernatural speculation and therefore creates a divorce between the experience and its conceptual expression. Whatever pictorial character apocalypticism still maintains, this pictorial character is reified and ontologized when actual historical persons are "apocalypticized," that is, when an actual historical person, Jesus, is transferred to that heavenly kingdom and is now viewed as a new heavenly substance, the Son of God sitting at the right hand of the Father. Thus the reification of apocalyptic language transmutes images into realities, and then the way is opened for metaphysical speculation. When Ernst Kasemann proclaims that apocalypticism is the mother of Christian theology, he is certainly correct. But his positive evaluation of this insight seems to be a possible tragedy. For the apocalyptic world view as the basic framework of interpreting Jesus seems to have facilitated the supernatural speculation of Christian dogma and has made it increasingly difficult for a nonmetaphysical age like ours to relate the biblical conceptuality to our experience. In some sense, the, metaphysical theology is philosophized apocalypticism. The myth is simply replaced by the philosophical concept.

Now it must be recognized that resurrection language is apocalyptic language; the resurrection is part and parcel of the apocalyptic world view and makes sense only in terms of it. The question is: If it proves impossible to resuscitate an apocalyptic world view, how shall we cope with the resurrection as an integral part of that world view? An honest consistency is demanded here. The fundamentalist who occupies essentially an apocalyptic world view is more honest and consistent than most Christians. For the fundamentalist believes both in the cosmic apocalyptic drama of the impending Parousia and in the resurrection of Christ as integrally connected, whereas most Christians are willing to demythologize the apocalyptic Parousia but refuse to do so with the equally apocalyptic resurrection of Christ because of its supposedly central New Testament character. And it is exactly the resurrection of Christ which shares the unintelligibility of the apocalyptic world view for modern man. Thus the resurrection of Christ hovers before us as an intellectual abstraction because we have no referent for it in our experience.

In this context recent scholarship seems to have sensed the divorce between the world of our experience and the theological concept. For the new quest of the historical Jesus in its investigation of the relation between the historical Jesus and the kerygmatic Christ senses that the era of the kerygmatic formula—however existentially pressed—is past: A kerygmatic conceptuality which is not grounded in the actual life of the historical Jesus is not convincing. In fact, the perennial quest for the historical Jesus seems to me to be a quest for the possibility of a religious stance within the world of human reality. However much the twentieth century from Albert Schweitzer on has mocked this quest of the historical Jesus as illegitimate and impossible, this should not blind our eyes to the fact that such a quest is our only way to Jesus himself as the source of all Christian religious perception. An experiential theology, however, must be careful not to confuse a quest of the historical Jesus with its own intention. For its intention is not a sketch of the Jesus of history "as he really was" but rather a quest for Jesus as he was *experienced* by his disciples and contemporaries. Jesus for experiential theology is the catalyst of a specific experience, not a unique superman or Son of God. Unless it is possible to trace the road from the experience men had with Jesus to their conceptual formulation of it—unless it is possible to trace the road by which Jesus became the Christ—the "Christ" remains an unintelligible concept to our world. This seems to be the only possible way that the apocalyptic conceptuality of the risen Christ can be translated meaningfully to us. For it is not the conceptuality which is crucial but the experience which expresses itself in various conceptualities; namely, the experience which men had with Jesus proved to be of such a character that they ascribed ultimacy to it—the ultimacy of God's final purpose with men, the ultimacy of Jesus as the Christ. The return to biblical New Testament religion, then, is conditioned by a return to the historical Jesus as the man who evokes faith and a new religious perception which alone provides the basis for all the subsequent interpretations by believers.

IV
TENTATIVE
CONCLUSION

If it is true that our age is deeply distrustful of metaphysics, ontology, and the ontological concept, and if it is likewise true that there is a renewed search for genuine experience as something a man can own and stand for, then there is no easy shortcut to the abiding experience of New Testament religion. The discontinuity of world views, the complex interaction between particular experiences and the particular world view of which these experiences are a part, make it exceedingly difficult to distill the "abiding" element in our contact with New Testament religion.

For the Christian, the return to New Testament religion is conditioned by a return to the historical Jesus as the originator of a new religious perception which provided the source for all subsequent theological interpretation. For all of the New Testament—in its understanding, misunderstanding, and broken-ness—testifies to the experiences people had with Jesus which proved to be of such a decisive nature that they confessed him as Christ and Son of God. This is not the place to argue the ultimate truth of Jesus' person and message for mankind. But at least it becomes possible to understand and give meaning to the claims the New Testament makes about Jesus. For through the least theological figure of the New Testament, the historical Jesus, we are able to trace the birth of religious perception and the particular focus it received in Jesus' passion for God and compassion for man. Only through the historical Jesus do we come to know the road from experience to interpretation, from the faith Jesus evoked to the christological interpretations which delineate the quality of that faith. And so we have the possibility to test whether the experience people had with Jesus *then* can still be our experience. For unlike the interpretative concept, unlike the doctrinal statement, unlike abstractions like the kerygma, the encounter with the historical Jesus executes a claim on our *experience,* since it does not ask from us ontological presuppositions as to Jesus' divine status. Unless the experiences which contemporaries had with Jesus are still a possibility for us, unless they have this abiding quality and can be distinguished from the particular apocalyptic conceptions of the surrounding world view, the return to the historical Jesus will be as meaningless as the bygone apocalyptic world view which surrounds him and informs so much the conceptuality of the New Testament.

Thus the return to New Testament religion as evocative of

religious experience is conditioned by a return to the historical Jesus as the one who not only occasioned all the *conceptuality* of the New Testament but who also may open the horizons of *our experience* in the modern world. If the concentration of theology on the ontological category and definition has become meaningless to us because of its lack of experiential verification, a return to biblical religion is the demand of the hour. Such a return to biblical religion is then only meaningful if we do not oversimplify the abiding element between the biblical experience and ours. Whatever the abiding element may prove to be, it is certain that it must be hooked into man's living experience and so constitute a genuine element of what it means to be fully human.

To confess Christ without Jesus is to equate a dogmatic abstraction without living experience. For unless we can travel the road by which Jesus became the Christ in early Christian experience, we cut the integral relation between experience and its conceptual formulation.

The road from living experience to its conceptual formulation in man's life parallels the road from the historical Jesus to the Christ of the kerygma. Gnosticism has always been the basic threat and enemy of Christianity. It faces us today in new forms and in a new radical way. For modern man who desires to make his stance in his felt experience of life simply asks whether orthodoxy in celebrating the dogmatic conceptuality apart from its grounding in man's experience has not in fact gnosticized the Christian experience. The danger of all Gnostic forms of Christianity is the desire to have a Christ without Jesus. Gnostic spirituality thus betrays the dignity of human life in this world and its concrete experience in the world. Because it posits a divine spark in man which has no contact with man's ordinary experience, it denies the value and dignity of man's felt experience. It displaces ordinary experiences for a series of extraordinary experiences, granted to an elite, practicing a conscious schizophrenia with the world. Thus, whether in terms of abstract formulations or of supernatural entities, every "Christ" who is not firmly grounded in one's experience of the man of Galilee must be rejected as endangering the dignity of man and his historical experience.

By necessity this chapter has been explorative in nature. It is intended to voice some of the questions facing any theologian today and to indicate a new direction for reshaping Christian theology. Clearly no concrete proposals for this new direction have been suggested. But there is gain in knowing that an updating of the old approaches will not do. Both historical positivism and kerygmatic theology are unable to resurrect Christian theology. A return to biblical religion is suggested here because it opens possibilities to find an experiential bridge between the biblical world and ours. Such an experiential bridge appeals to man's being in the world and to man's world of perceptions and resists appeals to extraordinary supernatural levels of being which must be accepted in advance. The following chapters will attempt to clarify in more detail this experiential approach to Christian theology.

The genuineness of the experiential bridge must be tested against the legitimate objections of the sociology of knowledge which have made us aware of the interrelation between world view conceptuality and experience. It must also be tested against the historical-critical objections of form criticism, which tends to argue that any approach to the relation between the historical Jesus and his disciples, i.e., to the historical Jesus as experienced by his disciples, is both illegitimate and impossible.

However, if such objections cannot be met, Christianity can no longer appeal to Jesus as the Christ and is forced to admit that some version of a Gnostic Christ is all that can be appealed to—and that human life and experience cannot be religious without blindly accepting some sort of esoteric revelation.

part two

Outline of
a Theology of
Experience

growth in response to jesus: toward an experiential theology based on existential phenomenology

C. DANIEL BATSON

Theology is now rapidly emerging from a nearly half-century-long period in which any attention to actual human experience was derogated. The history especially of Protestant theology from the publication of Karl Barth's *Epistle to the Romans* in the early 1920's up to the most recent years tells the story of the rediscovery of Biblical and Reformation objectivity. Barth insisted, especially in his early years, that subjectivity and human experience provided at best a deceptive basis for faith and a mercurial object for theology. The theologians, he insisted, must focus on the Word of God. Friedrich Schleiermacher, the great nineteenth-century theologian of experience, fell into disrepute. What was often somewhat arrogantly called "Biblical" theology became popular and no one paid much attention to human experience, religious or otherwise.[1]—Harvey Cox.

   As chapter 1 indicates, we are in agreement with Harvey Cox's sketch of the character of recent theology. The present task, however, is to go beyond an awareness of recent shortcomings to a positive statement which can overcome these weaknesses. Accordingly, this chapter is an attempt to present a general outline of an experiential theology by building upon a particular philosophical base, existential phenomenology. In order to state the perspective clearly, it will be presented in a straightforward fashion without elaborate documentation and qualification. Once presented, it can be contrasted with other approaches to theologizing, and attention can be given to some of the general questions it raises.

I
OUTLINE OF AN
EXPERIENTIAL THEOLOGY

A

Aspects of the Experience of Christian Growth

As Cox implies, what seems needed is a theology which focuses upon man's religious experience rather than one which begins with the givenness of God's Word as revelatory of the nature of God, the nature of man, and their relationship. Like any other Christian theology Jesus is focal to our experiential theology, but his life and ministry are approached self-consciously through the eyes of man, specifically through the eyes of the follower over against whom Jesus stands and whom he challenges to a new life of love in the community of faith. The experienced Jesus, not the Jesus of creed or doctrine, is our concern.

What sort of experience does Jesus seem to evoke in others? What is common to experiences which can be called Christian? To a disappointingly large degree the answer must be that we do not know. The necessary data lie masked behind the centuries and the personal idiosyncrasies of the Gospel writers in responding to the social and cultural demands of their time. A general theme does, however, seem to emerge: *The Christian experience (both today and yesterday) involves radical change. Man is challenged to see his world in a new way, centrifugally rather than centripetally.*[2]

Man is called by the life and ministry of Jesus to reorient himself in his world. Rather than focusing centripetally in upon himself and his own status (whether it be religious, psychic, economic, political, or social status), man is called to thrust his gaze outward, centrifugally, extending concern to his fellowman. The radical change which is sought is perceptual in this sense. Man is called to see himself in relation to his environment in a new way and, through an integration of perception into action, to display a changed orientation to life. [3]

More must be said about the character of such a reorientation experience. Gestalt psychologists speak of one's perceptual orientation as a "set"; one is primed to see in a particular way. More recent developments in phenomenology, cognitive psychology, and the sociology of knowledge suggest that this perceptual organization or set is also the ground upon which conscious conceptual systems are built.[4] The set or orientation is spoken of as being formed by perceptual structures or dimensions. These structures provide the matrix in which one renders perceptual stimulation meaningful. Some structures seem to be universally shared by all persons without some physical defect, as is, for example, the organization of color perception along dimensions of hue, brightness, and saturation. When one considers the more complex stimulus patterns characteristic of our everyday experience, however, there is far less consensus as to what constitutes reality. It is not uncommon to be engaged in an enthusiastic discussion until an "Oh, is *that* what you mean by . . . ?" reveals that the participants actually live in different worlds. One can even track changes in his own reality. Few Americans today perceive the Soviet Union in the way they did ten years ago. They very structures we use to organize our perceptions of Russia seem to be quite different. Whereas ten years ago an American might think of Russia in terms of military power and threat, the dominant perception now is more in terms of political power and ability and interest in negotiations. The hotheaded saberswinging cossack has been replaced by the cool vodka-swigging statesman.

As these illustrations suggest, one is not normally aware of his perceptual structures. They are not the subject of thought, but rather the framework one uses to think with. In this way they are the framework of reality itself. The experience of Christian growth seems to involve a change or shift in these perceptual structures, and thereby in one's very reality. One sees and understands himself and his world in a new way.

It was suggested that Christian experience involves radical perceptual change. "Radical" is a loaded term today, so care must be taken to specify how it is being used. Basically, in describing the perceptual shift as radical, the intent is to emphasize its *discontinuity* with the individual's prior perception of himself and his world. The experience involves not just adding new data or new interpretations to one's current perceptual structures (new wine into old wineskins) but involves a change of the structures themselves. Since the perceptual structures are themselves the very foundation upon which reflected, rational, logical thought is constructed, they are by definition nonlogical (not, of course, antilogical). Thus, one cannot track a change in these structures in a conscious, rational manner. It occurs abruptly, serendipitously.

For example, at a relatively trivial level, Gestalt psychologists have long pointed to the nonlogical shift of perceptual structures involved in a figure-ground reversal. What do you see in this figure? A vase . . . or two faces? As you stare at the figure, it will shift abruptly and without apparent effort from one figure to the other. What was the background becomes the figure, and vice versa. A  new "world" or "reality" is created. Since they require different organizations, one cannot see both figures at once. At a given time, one must live with one reality or the other, not both.

The type of nonlogical perceptual shift which occurs here seems to occur in a far more pervasive and personally significant manner in Christian experience. The Christian shift involves not just one's immediate perceptual set but the basic perceptual structures undergirding his whole reality. Further, a figure-ground reversal is simply a "flip" from one perceptual set to another. In contrast, Christian experience seems to involve a shift which transcends the current perceptual structures, producing movement outward away from exclusive self-concern. It is, I think, in this vein that Paul speaks of the "new creation" and the passage of the old (2 Corinthians 5:17). This transcendent quality allows one to speak of the experience as growth. It produces a new way of life, the natural expression of an outward or centrifugal rather than centripetal concern.

Finally, implicit within a perceptual shift is the discovery of the necessary limitation of one's view of the world, his reality. When one's reality changes, the possibility emerges for recognizing the limitation of any given perspective. If one simply flips to another absolute reality, another ideology, he has missed one of the basic lessons of such an experience, that our "truth" is only partial and relative, never absolute. Such a recognition evokes humility and openness to future change.

To summarize thus far, three aspects of Christian experience have been noted: (1) radical perceptual change leading to (2) a new reality involving (3) a new way of life. As a shorthand notation we shall speak of this entire process as a *perceptual shift*. The psychodynamics of this process will be discussed in more detail in chapter 3. For the present, it remains to suggest how Jesus is related to this growth process and what the characteristics of this new life seem to be, that is, how it is explicitly Christian.

Impetus. In Christian experience the life and ministry of Jesus provide the impetus for radical perceptual shifts. Jesus' method of bringing about such changes seems to have been through a two-pronged message. Most striking as one first reads the accounts of his ministry in the Gospels is his *confrontational challenge* to the existing religious and ethical interpretations of his day. "You have heard of old . . . , but I say unto you . . . ." So saying, he both articulates and challenges the perceptual structures undergirding the reality of his listeners. He continually forces one to go behind the meaning of the specific words or concepts one holds dear to the broader implications which, when matched with one's behavior, call for a radical reconception of one's life in relation to his social world. This juxtaposition of themes from the current reality and one's lived experience forces one to confront the contradictions or "cracks" in his reality. He can no longer live comfortably in his present world. Thus, Jesus challenged any superficial interpretation of the law, the focus of religious and ethical concern in Israel at that time, on the basis of the deeper meaning of the law, continually driving listeners to view the law and its implications for their lives in a new way.[5]

A subtler second element in Jesus' confrontation is also present in the Gospels; he provides a supportive context, both culturally (in language and conception) and socially, for those he challenges. Concerning language, the challenge to a more radical understanding of the law was in the context of an intimate and personal view of God as *abba*, the father of a family.[6] This accepting interpretation of the key religious symbol, God, freed the existent religious language from much of its judgmental character, allowing it to function supportively for the thought and expression of the man of faith. Socially, Jesus created a community into which one could move to live out the new perceptions evoked by Jesus' challenge. This community, a collection of "publicans and sinners," consists of those who have given up all pretense of making themselves righteous before divine justice. Acceptance and support is offered to those who no longer seek to justify or "save" themselves but to respond to the needs of others. The social and cultural contexts interact; the social context, the church, uses the language of faith, and the language shapes the church.[7]

Thus, Jesus confronts those who will listen and challenges them to change radically in a context of support. This is the milieu of the perceptual shift which is Christian growth. If either side of this two-pronged message is lost, the creative impetus of the message suffers. Challenge without support becomes threatening judgment; support without challenge, a secure womb.

Direction. Jesus also points the direction in which one is called to change. As has been noted, his concern seems to have been not just for a changed outlook but for a perceptual shift which manifests itself in *action*. Unidimensional emphases on either radical change or responsible action have been frequent in Christendom, especially in debates over personal salvation or regeneration versus social action. Emphasis has been either upon a changed life or upon ethical principles. Rather than this either/or, however, the shift Jesus tries to evoke seems to involve reintegration and reorientation of life *toward* ethical action. This unity of purpose requires a more profound response than does emphasis on either side of the polarity.

On the one hand, Jesus' listeners are not challenged simply to a reconception of the law within an existing conceptual framework of personal salvation. They are challenged to alter that framework and the salvation-seeking behavior it generates altogether. The search for salvation itself is revealed to be a self-centered quest. The Christian is reborn, but not into personal salvation. Rather, he loses interest in this concern altogether.[8] Yet, on the other hand, the alternative is not adherence to a set of ethical principles. The Christian message comes not as a demand that one accept and adhere to certain moral rules, to a Christian perspective on issues, or to a Christian life-style. To change one's outlook radically in response to Jesus' challenge involves movement toward a free expression of ethical action, not conformity. Thus, Christian growth is in the direction of responsible action, not toward right thinking which one then feels obliged to implement.[9]

The action to which Jesus calls one is not, however, just any action. The radical change is in a particular direction. It is, first, action based upon a perception of one's relationship to others as "neighbor." As one grows as a Christian, his gaze is less cast down or to "the other side of the road." It falls more fully upon the needs of his fellowman, recognizing his needs as needs, not as interesting or disgusting quirks or even as facts of the human situation.

Implicit in Jesus' emphasis upon being neighbor is a concern to meet another in his own reality. As with Zacchaeus, Jesus' concern does not seem to involve a preconceived notion of what a person needs but instead a sensitivity to the whole situation, including the person's own perception of himself and the situation. Yet, to translate being neighbor into "doing whatever anyone wants me to do" is too simple. It ignores both the multiplicity of demands operative in any given situation and the real possibility that a person may have either a distorted view of or ambivalence about his own needs. A person may seek aid which reinforces dependence, for this is more comforting than a loving challenge toward liberation and growth. Often only in retrospect can we recognize and accept concern which goes beyond the surface to deal with deeper and actually more basic needs. Finally, to grow in this direction means that one perceives an increasing number of people as neighbors. It is easy to extend such concern to family or friends, but Jesus' challenge is to widen this circle to include more and more people—poor, rich, black, white, oppressor or oppressed.

This first directive is the challenge toward *outwardness*, the extension of one's gaze outward to see the needs of one's fellowman as one's own and to respond to them as such. This process seems to be one of expansion of one's need awareness, not of substitution of others' needs for one's own. Jesus challenges one to grow toward being a committed "neighbor."

Second, and correlative to this first directive, Jesus challenges one to face the uncertainties and ambiguities of his own reality, recognizing its limitations and being ready to change perceptions on the basis of further information. In this way Jesus dethrones ideology. This is the call to *openness*.[10] To be free from ideological calcification, one's reality must remain supple, in tune with his experience. Out of new experiences, new realities should be born. Exemplary of such openness is Jesus' continual reevaluation of the scope and nature of his own ministry as, for example, in the encounter with the Canaanite woman (Matthew 15:21ff.).

The Christian is called to be an uneasy bedfellow of any cause. He cannot assume that he knows what is right. To be open to changes in one's perceptions and to the relativity of one's interpretations, to refuse to ideologize, is not, however, a cop-out on ethical responsibility. Not only does the Christian as "neighbor" find himself committed to action. He finds he must take increased responsibility for his action, for he cannot assume the accuracy of his own stance. He finds himself increasingly aware of the limitation and finitude of his own view and of his need to attempt to read and respond sensitively to as many aspects of each situation as possible. In *The Responsible Self* H. Richard Niebuhr has reminded us that this is what responsibility entails. Unquestioning ideological devotion or submission to a moral code is irresponsible; it imposes one's reality on others and denies openness to new experiences and information.

Thus, Jesus' challenge is, though directive, open-ended. The Christian is involved in a continual growth or change process in the context of the basic shift of extending his concern beyond himself. This ongoing growth process not only affects his behavior in specific situations but also requires continual reexamination of his commitment to any specific cause or ideology. As with Jesus himself, where this direction will lead him the Christian cannot say. Because he lacks the security of a firm ideology, he has no Celestial City toward which he marches. But he does not experience this as a loss. Rather he finds himself so caught up in the needs of those around him that residence in such a city, should it exist, seems decidedly uninteresting (see the parables of the kingdom, especially Matthew 25:31-46).

Finally, in pointing to these two directives, outwardness and openness, it is by no means to be assumed that we have exhausted the concerns expressed by Jesus in his life and ministry. These two strike us as the most obvious and most consistently central, and their scope is by no means small. But to absolutize them into necessary and exclusive norms for the Christian life is far from our intent.

B
Theological Furniture
In outline form this seems to be the character of the experience of Christian growth, a perceptual shift in the directions of outwardness and openness in response to the challenge of Jesus. Something must now be said about the status of this interpretation as a theological statement. Anyone acquainted with contemporary Christian theology, especially discussions of man since Reinhold Niebuhr's *The Nature and Destiny of Man,* may well have experienced a growing sense of unease in reading this outline. Not only would much of what has been said be affirmed by prior treatments of what it means to be Christian by neo-orthodox and what might be called post-neo-orthodox theologians[11] (though in different terms), their discussions include so much more! Our new theological house seems to be furnished with bricks and boards and little else.

Totally missing are such basic appointments of neo-orthodox explications of man's Christian experience as the *imago Dei,* the fall, the relation of *pneuma* and *sarx,* attention to Jesus the Christ as the embodiment of true humanity—the list could be extended much farther. Also absent are post-neo-orthodox conceptions of Christian life such as Harvey Cox's secular Christianity, William Hamilton's Christian humanism, Norman Pittenger's moral being, and even Sam Keen's *homo tempestivus.* All of these concepts are missing because each concerns a

Christian view of the nature of man, and nothing has been said here about the nature of man at all.

Perhaps even more disturbing, nothing has been said about the nature of God and the God-man relationship. These rooms have been left totally bare. True, Jesus' association of the symbol "God" with *abba* was noted, but no emphasis has been placed on God as an active agent. There is no mention of his triune nature, of his active involvement in a redeeming salvation history, or of his proleptic (Pannenberg) or eschatalogical relation to history (Moltmann), even of his kenotic death (Altizer). There is no talk of the divine-human relationship (Barth), the ground of Being (Tillich), the God at the center (Bonhoeffer), or the "beyond in the midst" (J.A.T. Robinson). Nor, indeed, is the placement of God within a process metaphysic entertained (cf. Hartshorne, Cobb, and Williams). Finally, the gospel is not conceived as either an existential *kerygma* (Bultmann) or a "Word event" (the new hermeneuticians).

At the risk of setting the unsettled mind more on edge than at ease, it must be emphasized that these exclusions are intentional. Our furnishing has been purposely sparse. Questions and statements concerning the nature of God, man, and the God-man encounter, the customary centerpieces of Christian theology, seem to be unnecessary and even potentially dangerous frills. And the same is true of the more recent concern to build Christian theologies or views "of" various concepts such as revolution, history, hope, or play. When one begins theologizing from Christian experience using a phenomenological orientation, such questions and concerns never arise. More importantly, they are little missed, since it seems that Jesus challenges man to a new reality and new action, not new understanding. And each of these views "of" seem oriented toward new understanding.

It is true that certain biblical writers give considerable attention to issues of the nature of God, man, and their relationship (most notably the authors of the *J* creation account in Genesis, the Johannine Gospel, and several of the Pauline letters). But to feature these passages to the relative exclusion of the mainstream of less reflective historical writings one finds in much of the Pentateuch, in the prophetic and wisdom literature of the Old Testament, and in the Synoptic Gospels in the New Testament seems misguided. Jesus' ministry, as presented in the Synoptics, seems geared toward the dethronement of precisely such credos with their ideological descriptions of true reality. He challenges us to move beyond their security. Why then are they so central to recent theological discussions?

As the statement by Harvey Cox quoted at the beginning of this chapter suggests, Karl Barth seems to have set the stage for the recent emphasis on Christian views of reality and thereby for Christian ideologies (the roots could, of course, be traced much farther back). Although he expressly intended to develop a theology without making any philosophical presuppositions, his conceptual framework of the radical distance between man and God in his early works, the total depravity of man, and of theology as the science of God's living Word revealed in Jesus Christ presupposes a grand metaphysical drama of salvation.[12] Barth claims we can only know about man by looking at Jesus Christ, the "true man" (cf. Paul Tillich's similar emphasis upon Jesus the Christ as the New Being in his conquest of estrangement of human essence and existence), and the truth which is revealed is principally in terms of a description of "human nature" in both its sinful and redeemed states. Reinhold Niebuhr operates in a parallel manner. His treatment of the Christian view of man as both higher and lower than other views remains focused on a description of what man is, of human nature. What seems to be unintentionally subverted in each of these attempts to present the Christian view of man is the dynamic thrust of the challenge for ethical and religious change and responsible action which Jesus places before each of us. Christian experience becomes encapsulated within a metaphysical theology, within a statement about reality. And cast as a metaphysical theology, it becomes an ideology—a truth which, while designed to give illumination and freedom, actually enslaves.

But certainly these theologians did not intend such a distortion. They, like us, sought to understand what it means to be Christian. Why, then, such a gap between the intent and the result? The slippage appears most clearly at the level of language; a mixture of "language games" (to use Ludwig Wittgenstein's phrase) seems to have occurred. The philosophical assumptions undergirding most Western theologies appear to have inadvertently shaped their interpretation of Christian language. And metaphysical philosophy, whether idealist, realist, existential, or process, is concerned to describe and explain reality. When one approaches either Christian experience today or as expressed in the biblical record from the perspective of one of these philosophies, it is only natural to assume that the symbolic religious language the Christian speaks is also an attempt to describe or explain reality. But ironically, to emphasize the descriptive and explanatory aspects of the biblical language moves one inextricably into a different language game from the ethical-action language which seems so central to the Bible. Once one has set Man for the Bible in the context of a metaphysical system of Finitude in separation from an Infinite God due to Sin (note the telltale ontological capitals), it seems quite difficult to read the Gospel in terms other than as a metaphysical transaction of salvation.

Was such a message intended? If it is true, as many philosophers of religious language now argue, that Christian language is not primarily reflective but convictional in function, the answer is probably no.[13] To illustrate the difference, consider the usage of an ancient confessional statement. Rather than responding to "Jesus is Lord" with "What does that mean?" or "Prove it!," as appropriate in a metaphysical descriptive-explanatory language game, the response in a commitment-action game would seem to be, after reflection, either "yes" or "no" (commitment) and, if yes, "What now do I do about it?" (action).[14] Christian language seems to be used primarily in this latter fashion, except by those interested in theological debate. In lived Christian experience it is not used to describe or point to some aspect of reality. Not referential, it is symbolic, being used in an attempt to express and evoke an experience.

If this commitment-action emphasis is central to Christian language, it seems obvious that it should be reflected in any Christian theology. Instead, however, the experience which the theologian has sought to understand seems to have been subverted by the understanding itself. Attention has actually been directed away from Christian experience, responsible action being replaced by theological reflection. And this has led to the rather awkward situation in which we find ourselves today, in which it is difficult to speak of the ethical and religious life of the Christian except as "doing theology."

To distinguish the commitment-action language of faith from the descriptive-explanatory language of theological reflection only serves to reveal the theologian's dilemma. As an intellectual enterprise, theology must use a reflective language. But, to be true to the experience it is seeking to illumine, this language must evoke understanding of the dynamics of faith rather than shifting the emphasis away from the "commitment action" of faith. Is it possible to reflect without distorting the gospel's actional thrust? As suggested in chapter 1, the first step toward clarity is certainly to recognize that religious faith and theology are not synonymous. One can be religious without being very theological (Jesus seems to fall into this category), and, indeed, while one is being theological it even seems doubtful whether it is possible for him to be actively religious. The current meld of religious experience with theology as a result of the neo-orthodox reaction to liberalism's use of the term religion seems to court a dangerous cerebration of faith. The commitment-action thrust is easily swallowed by conceptualization. The second step is to choose one's philosophical foundation for theological reflection carefully.

C
Philosophical Foundation

The philosophical foundation on which one builds his theological house determines the shape of the entire structure. One cannot think without making assumptions of a philosophical sort, assumptions as to what is, what is knowable and how, and what is of value. But if one's assumptions for his thought are at odds with the character of the experience one seeks to understand, one undermines his own intent. It is because the assumptions of existential phenomenology seem more consonant with the commitment-action dynamic of the Christian gospel than do the idealist, realist, existential, or process assumptions which have dominated recent theology that we have chosen this philosophical base. We believe that a theology based on existential phenomenology may allow for greater understanding and less misunderstanding of Christian experience, the goal of any theology. No doubt existential phenomenology also can, should, and will be supplanted by even more appropriate philosophical bases for Christian theology, but at present it seems to suggest a most promising step in the right direction.

How does a base in existential phenomenology overcome the gap between Christian experience and theological reflection which has plagued so much Christian theology? First, the phenomenologist recognizes it. He recognizes that the "natural attitude," the world of distinction of subject and object, of language and of concepts, the everyday world in which we naturally move, is a constructed world, built upon a more "primordial" level of unreflected lived experience. Intertwined with the visible of this experience (visible in that one is at once both seer and seen) is the invisible, unconscious structures or dimensions (which Maurice Merleau-Ponty, following Edmund Husserl, calls "horizon structures") with which we experience meaningfully even at this primordial, unreflected level. These are the perceptual structures discussed earlier. This primordial level should not be equated with the subjective, for it is presubjective as well as preobjective. The subject-object dichotomy, the nemesis which seems to lead to idealist and realist quests for true reality, is not overcome in an *a posteriori* Hegelian synthesis but in a primordial "passive synthesis." Nor should primordial experience be considered as the individual's passive acceptance of the "sense data" from the world; rather, it is active experiencing itself. To emphasize the presubjective and preobjective nature of this experience as well as its active, dynamic character, one might say: Our world-experiencing is necessarily meaningful (or, with Merleau-Ponty, "condemned to meaning") because of the intentionality of our perceptual structures.

Merleau-Ponty emphasizes perception as being the best channel for apprehension of the primordial, since perceptual structures make meaningful our unreflected experience of the world. As outlined previously, to change perceptual structures involves an abrupt, translogical jump (such as the figure-ground reversal in Gestalt psychology) and results in "seeing" oneself and one's world anew. Again following Husserl, Merleau-Ponty notes that our perceptions, our judgments, indeed, our whole knowledge of the world can be changed or "crossed out," but it cannot be nullified. We shift from one primordial meaning to another but are condemned by the structure of incarnate consciousness to have some meaning.[15]

This general philosophical framework suggests both the limitation and potential of theological language. Because our language is founded upon the subject-object dichotomy of the natural attitude, the phenomenologist recognizes that it cannot apprehend primordial experience directly. Experience at the primordial level can only be spoken of through an indirect affirmation-negation process with regard to any specific conceptual content. That is, in attempting to speak of the primordial, one must be ready to negate each affirmation, using the language dialectically to evoke an understanding of an experience, beyond and behind language. One says what it is, only to contradict himself quickly and assert that what he has just said is not it.[16] This affirmation-negation technique forces one to recognize the symbolic, nonreferential way the language is being used.

Similarly, the theologian must be ready to use his concepts in an "odd" way.[17] Since the dynamic which he is seeking to interpret does not operate at a rational level but involves a shift at the primordial level in one's entire perceptual framework, it seems necessary for the theologian to use his language "lightly" or "playfully." This does not, of course, mean that he takes what he is doing lightly, but that he recognizes that whatever he says is never in itself correct. He must maintain the tension between the experiential dynamic which he is attempting to describe and the rational level of his description. If one were to propose a paradigm of such a theological method, Dostoevski's chapter in *The Brothers Karamazov* on "The Grand Inquisitor" serves admirably. The depth of the experience of Christian freedom and responsibility is laid bare as the dialogue between Ivan and Alyosha unwinds. In contradicting logical meanings and destroying the discursive function of the language, a feeling for the experience is evoked.

When the theologian begins to treat religious symbols such as God referentially, assuming they point to something or someone beyond human experience, an ideology with its absolutes is born. But when one recognizes that man's linguistic and conceptual categories are not images of a reality "out there" but involve rational construction upon primordial experience, ideological concern to infuse confidence into one's knowledge of the world by absolutizing disappears. Indeed, as one recognizes the multiplicity of perceptual structures and of the rational processes operating within these, he finds the quest for Absolute Reality of a metaphysical sort uninteresting, if not suspect. One simply cannot "jump out of his skin" to see himself in relation to his world or even to God from a third-person point of view; the categories of "self," "world," and "God" are themselves abstract objectifications upon primordial experiencing. Certainly man can and must objectify in an attempt to make sense out of his primordial experience, but to allow such objectification to occur without attention to the primordial experience upon which the "objective" categories are based seems misguided. The phenomenologist's concern is thus to deal responsibly with the tension between the logical "reality" of everyday world and the a-logical or prelogical level of primordial experience, recognizing both and their interaction without reducing one into the other.

As outlined here, Christian experience seems to participate in this tension. One is challenged to change his perceptual structures themselves at the primordial level so that his very experiencing and his reality change. But the change also affects life in the everyday world of the natural attitude—not through specification of the nature of the world into which one is to move but through a continual challenge to one's current conceptions of his world in the context of support (i.e., the society and culture of the church). The Christian hope is not in a given concept or event but in a direction, an opening movement outward in loving concern for one's neighbor. The earlier insistence on both radical personal change and responsible action can now be seen to be a unitary process occurring at two levels: a breakdown or cracking of one's present reality results in (1) a change in the primordial perceptual structures which creates (2) a new life in the world of the natural attitude.

Two traditional theological concepts, transcendence and sin, deserve some comment in light of this phenomenological foundation. If one maintains an experiential perspective, transcendence seems to be experienced not in moving to an absolute, ultimate, or essential metaphysical level but in transcending beneath and behind the natural attitude of everyday life to allow for creative restructuring of one's reality. As reality is re-formed in harmony with lived experience, the old enslaving reality is transcended. The proposed a-metaphysical phenomenological position takes no stand on the question of the existence or nonexistence of a transcendent realm, this issue being left open and unresolved. Focusing instead upon the Christian experience of transcendence, one finds it to be a human process for which Jesus is the impetus. The goal of such transcendence is not movement out of the everyday world but movement into the world in a new way. Is there a metaphysical dimension beyond or behind or within us to which such transcendent experiences allude? Or, more pointedly, does God exist? Again maintaining the experiential focus, one must answer each question, "We need not, and perhaps cannot, know." Such knowledge is not necessary for the Christian gospel to function creatively.

This experiential approach to transcendence can be contrasted with two other phenomenological uses of the term. First, Peter Berger's *A Rumor of Angels,* though hinting at a treatment similar to that proposed here, seems in the end to be a concern for a transcendent realm. His "signals of transcendence" are pointers away from experience toward a transcendent reality, a supernatural. Also, Langdon Gilkey's use of transcendence in *Naming the Whirlwind* seems finally referential, pointing to a real beyond, albeit a beyond within human experience, an "ultimate dimension." Gilkey's concern is to relate "religious discourse to concrete and contemporary experience without sacrificing either its biblical or traditional content, its transcendent reference, or its possibility of intelligible ontological and cultural explication."[18]

In challenging the understanding of phenomenology which lies behind Gilkey's analysis, I by no means wish to detract from the immense contribution his work makes toward exploration of the potential of phenomenology as a basis for a positive rather than simply reactive (i.e., post-neo-orthodox) contemporary theology. His argument seems a struggle within itself between a phenomenological concern to theologize from the religious experience and to use religious language as a symbolic expression of this experience on the one hand and an assertion of an ultimate or sacred dimension within ordinary experience and a God beyond-within, reminiscent of Tillich's ground of Being, on the other.

The present position would also seem to suggest that sin be seen in a new way. Rather than centering upon sin as an element in a cosmological drama of salvation, something which all received at the fall and has been atoned for by the Incarnate Crucified Christ, sin can be viewed experientially as the narrowness of man's reality which prevents him from acting responsibly in his social environment. This would seem to be the basis for Jesus' separation of the sheep from the goats (Matthew 25:31ff.). In such a view one's recognition of sin is an unending process so long as one is growing. For as our horizons of responsibility broaden, we become aware of their prior narrowness. Truly, then, we are called to "sin boldly." For sin is not something from which one escapes, except by stopping to grow; it is where one continually recognizes oneself to have been as one grows in the directions of outwardness and openness. In traditional theological categories the present focus is upon sanctification (in the sense of loving response, not internal purity) far more than justification.

II
SOME QUESTIONS RAISED
BY THE PROPOSED
EXPERIENTIAL THEOLOGY

Clearly, this theological stance raises many questions and reservations, only a few of which can be briefly considered here. *First, can it really be said that Christian language is predominantly a-metaphysical, and if so does this not eliminate the need for Christian theology?* Care must be taken in asserting that Christian language is predominantly a-metaphysical for it is quite clear that biblical writers raise numerous complex metaphysical questions, questions certainly worthy of pursuit. Yet, and this is the point, the biblical writer usually seems incredibly uninterested in them. One is often appalled at the lack of reflective analysis and systematization offered to support assertions made. The reason, as has been suggested, seems to be that usually the writer is not attempting to make a metaphysical point but to evoke a commitment-action response. Thus, for example, to Moses' question as to whom he shall say sent him, an "I am that I am" is sufficient (Exodus 3:14).[19]

But in suggesting this distinction between the commitment-action core of the biblical message and the less central rational reflective motifs, are we not led into a position such as Søren Kierkegaard's where the separation between subjective and objective truth (or between committed faith and theological reflection) is so great that even if the biblical record should be totally disproven to reason it would be of no consequence for the man of faith? That is, cannot one simply divorce the commitment action of Christian language from the conceptual exigencies of theological reflection? If the basic thrust of the Christian message is to generate action through a new vision, what matter if the basis for the vision seems either internally contradictory or totally lacking? The matter is clearly considerable, for unless the Christian message speaks responsibly to us where we are as reflective as well as actional beings, it cannot speak at all. If it can be "falsified," its creative power is undercut.[20] As psychology has made clear, human volition is not independent of cognition.

In addition to protection against falsification, theology has a positive function for the man of faith. Although theological reflection should not be substituted for the commitment-action language of faith, it can direct one's usage of such language so that its commitment-action function may be realized. It may provide a guide enabling one to "rightly divide the word of truth," accenting its regenerative, nonreferential character. How this is done is a dominant concern of the remaining chapters of this book.

Turning to a second basic question raised by our thesis and explication: Why Jesus? That is, if one is talking about radical personal change leading to ethical action, why focus on Jesus as the initiator of the process? When one lays aside the trappings of a cosmology of the Incarnate Christ saving man from sin, this question becomes crucial.

Indeed, in the context of our a-metaphysical experiential theology it does not seem possible to answer this question in a logically satisfying manner. Any answer must come, not in terms of a general argument pointing to some unique characteristic of Jesus' personality, nature, or even his self-understanding. These are not at issue: they lie well beyond our grasp. Experientially, one can only answer in terms of his own response to the challenge (both in speech and action) with which Jesus' life and ministry confronts him. He can affirm, if true, that many questions which the writers of the Gospels portray Jesus as sharpening for those to whom he spoke and ministered are important questions for him in his present situation: questions of how, if at all, to serve one's neighbor; of one's relation to the existing moral code; of how one lives meaningfully in his world; of death, and so on. But experientially, in response to such questions one cannot prove that Jesus' challenge must be the impetus for religious growth, for the growth experience itself is not one of logical deduction. It is primordial and prelogical. If Jesus does not sharpen key questions for a given individual, for him the answer is simply "not Jesus."

This is not to say that one adopts a take-it-or-leave-it attitude. More than once Jesus wept over the lack of response. But the necessity of response cannot be demonstrated. One must ultimately respond to the "why?" question as Philip responded to Nathanael: "Come and see (John 1:46)." As Jesus himself suggested in the parable of the sower, for some people he simply may not speak to them in their world. If not, his words are not "good news." For others, the threat of his challenge may be too great to allow response. For them, his word is judgment and a cause for sorrow. For others, his words are indeed "gospel." Therefore, to the question "Why Jesus?" the answer of the man of faith can only be, "He speaks to me and to others, come and see if he speaks to you."[21]

Because one cannot rationally demonstrate the significance of the experienced impetus for Christian growth, the experience maintains a quality of mystery. To express this mystery one resorts to appellatives such as those applied to Jesus: "the Christ," "Messiah," "Son of God," or "Son of man." The Christian affirms that Jesus' words (and actions) are the Word of God or of Life (Logos). In so saying, the major concern of the speaker does not seem to be to make grand metaphysical claims. Rather, he resorts to symbols to express the mystery of his experienced encounter with Jesus. It should be clear that from our experiential perspective such symbols are by no means to be regretted in the language of faith. They are the very center of this language, growing out of and affirming the mystery of the power of Jesus to effect change. The nature of the change process at the primordial level is necessarily beyond the grasp of any discursive language. Symbols appear to have the affirmation-negation process "built in" and thus have the potential for allowing the mystery of faith arising from Jesus' challenge to be recognized and not reduced.[22]

For many, to affirm the mysterious flavor of religious experience is unsatisfying. Why? The dissatisfaction seems to be based on assuming that religious language is referential, that it actually points to or describes something. Within such a language game, if one cannot specify the referent and so invokes mystery, questions must be raised as to whether anything is really being said. Whatever is being discussed seems illusory. But this suspicion dissolves when one recognizes that religious language is not referential. Symbolic language does not attempt to point to some phenomenon but to evoke an understanding, appreciation, and perhaps re-creation of a lived experience. And the language of mystery has a necessary and constructive function in such an attempt; it helps express the transcendence and significance of the experience.

An additional answer to the "Why Jesus?" question on a more pragmatic level must be noted briefly. Jesus' ministry resulted in the creation of a community and a language system (Christian language and theological reflection upon it) which can function both to stimulate and to provide support and interpretation as one seeks meaningful expression of an experience of growth in the directions of outwardness and openness. For many, their involvement with this community, the church, is the most direct answer to the "Why Jesus?" question. The Christian community offers, at least in theory, a context for handling basic religious conflicts creatively. In addition to stimulation and support, the community provides a corrective to the possibility of purely personalistic responses to Jesus' call. Again, account must be taken of the tentative nature of our "reality" and the possibility of error (i.e., pathology) in our perceptual restructuring.

Given this answer to the second question, a third one arises: Does the interpretation proposed not lead to a Jesusolatry? For the Christian, one who experiences Jesus as Christ, Jesus is the one who speaks the Word of Life in a unique and definitive way. Yet, to say that Jesus is the only channel for the divine word of regeneration again demands that one jump outside himself into metaphysical pronouncements. Indeed, as our chapters 4 and 5 will demonstrate, the Old Testament gives ample evidence of the "divine word" which judges and renews coming from others besides Jesus. Thus, although the present focus is almost exclusively on Jesus, it seems excessive to suggest he is necessarily the only source of the Word of Life. If another finds the impetus for growth in the directions of outwardness and openness elsewhere—whether in the Old Testament, in modern art, literature, or music, in the thought of the Buddha, or in his day-to-day encounters—the Christian's response would seem only to be, "Praise the Lord!" One can only affirm that, as a Christian, Jesus is the paradigmatic source of this Word for him.

To attribute the exclusivist emphasis of much of the New Testament to Jesus himself seems unfounded. Although far from unconcerned that growth in the direction outlined as Christian take place, often in the Synoptics he seems strangely uninterested in his own role in the change process. He seems more concerned with repentance itself than with the source of that repentance (as in his encouraging the disciples to teach and heal).

With regard to the emphasis on Jesus for the Christian, however, perhaps more specific mention should be made of the almost total lack of attention given to Paul in the preceding pages. For Paul has been the focal figure for much Protestant theology, especially in recent years. It seems natural that the theologian should be drawn to the Pauline writings, for they are themselves primarily theological reflection and interpretation of Paul's religious experience rather than being directly religious. In the Gospels, on the other hand, especially the Synoptics, the dynamics and complexities of religious experience are more directly exposed. Given this difference (which receives far more attention in chapter 6), in an attempt to focus upon the Christian experience it seems necessary to move behind Paul's theology and attempt to approach the life and ministry of Jesus as experienced by those with whom he interacted. This is not to say that Paul is unimportant or has little to offer. Obviously he is and he does. Rather, the intent is simply to restore the focus of Christian theology where it must belong—on Jesus. The Protestant Pauline focus seems to be one of the major factors leading to the tendency previously noted for Christianity to be portrayed, at least in learned circles, as a metaphysical theology rather than an ethical religion.

Having considered the nature of the present emphasis upon Jesus, let us face the question of Jesusolatry, or worship of the man Jesus, more directly. To say that Jesus is the source of one's renewal should not result in worshiping Jesus, for Jesus is not here considered as an object but as a person who confronts, challenges, and comforts. He is not dealt with as a prototype for what man is (i.e., as exhibiting true human nature) or even for what man ought to be (i.e., as an example for true human action). Rather, he is the one who speaks through his word and action, challenging me toward responsible action in my present world. Again the focus is upon the man to whom Jesus speaks and who is called to answer.[23]

Revelation is seen in a new light in this context. Jesus is a source of revelation but is not himself the revelation. Through his challenge, our own contradictions and conflicts are revealed to us, leading to growth. Thus, revelation is considered in terms of a human process rather than specific content or even an act of God. Still, consistent with a major emphasis of traditional notions of revelation, the impetus for the process is outside the individual. The Christian finds himself revealed as *Jesus speaks.* The difference suggested is not simply a semantic one, for on it turns the focus of one's theology. The present conception remains directed toward the process of Christian growth within the man of faith. The alternative seems to be the traditional cosmological drama between the forces of Good and Evil in which man is basically reduced to a perhaps enraptured onlooker.

It should be clear that the position here proposed leads to a focal emphasis upon the life and ministry of Jesus rather than upon either his incarnation or his resurrection (as is common in the drama of the God-man interaction of metaphysical theologies). His basic significance lies in the Word of Life he speaks and acts. The significance of his existence and of his death is interpreted in the light of this basic emphasis rather than vice versa. The doctrines of incarnation and resurrection are seen to be theological reflection (and not integral to the commitment-action language of the Christian religion). They are legitimate and necessary reflection, to be sure, but, as reflection, their foundational source in the life and ministry of Jesus must not be lost. The human experience they were coined to express, not their historicity, seems crucial. Here as elsewhere our experiential theology does not suggest the addition or detraction of any elements from the Christian message or even from Christian theology, only a shifting of the relative emphasis in an attempt to rebalance the scales in the theological treatment of the Christian experience away from the conceptual and toward the dynamic.

Finally, it must be asked: What, if any, are the evaluative criteria which one applies to Christian growth to distinguish healthy Christian growth from pathology? As with any sociocultural phenomenon, the Christian community must exercise some evaluative restraint on its linguistic and social forms. Neither the language nor the experience can be treated simply as Rorschach ink blots onto which one projects whatever meaning he desires. But what evaluative criteria should be used? The community would seem to have two criteria to apply in evaluating Christian growth. The first is internal consistency. Does one participate in the Christian language system in a manner consistent with its original intent, to the degree that we know that intent? Christian language, being basically symbolic, seems to have considerable latitude in interpretation, allowing one to express the unique character of his own experience. There are, however, limits to how far the language can be pushed without its meaning being totally transformed and its creative potential lost. The community has the responsibility of preserving this potential of Christian language by maintaining some consistency in its use.

The second criterion is functional. If Christian growth is indeed in the direction of increased outwardness and openness expressed in responsible action, are there signs of such growth in the life of the Christian? If not, to speak of the experience as Christian seems meaningless. As Jesus makes clear in his parables of the kingdom ("when did we see you in prison . . . ?"), ethical action is integral to Christian growth. Therefore, it seems legitimate to ask of the Christian whether his behavior in his social environment expresses growth. The basic verification of Christian language is behavioral.

This functional criterion points to a broader implication of the growth emphasis of the proposed experiential theology. Using medical categories, it should be clear that what is being proposed is a theology of health, not of sickness. Characteristic of post-Freudian and postexistential theology has been an acute awareness of man's anxiety, despair, meaninglessness, and general "sickness." To modern man's anguished cries for help the Christian gospel is proffered. It can provide personal identity, meaning, acceptance, an overcoming of estrangement. Such theologies of pathology, though certainly sensitive in describing the plight of modern man (at least from the perspective of several major anthropologies), tend to maintain the focus of concern on the individual's personal salvation, on one's recovery of meaning and purpose in life. Although the nature of the concern for personal salvation is quite different from that of the fundamentalist, the concern remains.

But, as has been suggested, one of the major themes of Jesus' ministry seems to have been to challenge the very concern for personal salvation—"whoever would save his life will lose it (Mark 8:35)." Perhaps as a result of a changing mood in psychology away from a rather exclusive focus on pathology toward increased interest in healthy, growing behavior (produced in large part by Abraham Maslow), it now seems possible to challenge the focus on pathology and survival in theology. Accordingly, the proposed experiential theology assumes, as Jesus seems to have, that the individual is capable of and should be challenged toward positive growth beyond simple survival. One is challenged to move beyond himself in concern for others and in openness to further change. The Christian gospel is not presented as a lifesaver. Rather, it involves a positive mandate to live for others.

One may respond to these assertions with the next line of the saying just quoted, "whoever loses his life . . . will save it," arguing that Jesus really was concerned with personal salvation. Such an assertion, however, seems to miss the significance of the order in which the two clauses appear. The order suggests that personal salvation may occur—personal identity and meaning may be obtained—through losing oneself, but only as a by-product. To interpret the passage as revealing the trick to gaining salvation would seem to be a serious misreading. Rather, in losing oneself to others in service, identity and meaning may be serendipitously bestowed. Salvation as traditionally understood is not a goal of Christian experience, only a gracious by-product. Indeed, this surprise benefit would seem to be the experiential meaning of what is traditionally spoken of as God's grace. But to come to Jesus seeking salvation as did the rich young man (Mark 10:17ff.) is to ask to have your question turned on you, away from salvation toward service.

To conclude, the thematic core of the proposed experiential theology is: In response to Jesus' life and ministry one may find his reality changed through perceptual shifts, changed away from an exclusive focus inward upon his own needs toward growth in the directions of outwardness of concern and openness to further change. In addition to explicating this thesis and placing it in the context of contemporary theology, I have attempted to deal with some of the more general questions which it raises.

Numerous other very complex questions are, of course, raised by the experiential approach to theology suggested here, questions which must be answered if this approach is to be taken seriously. Many of these will be addressed in the subsequent chapters. To list but a few: First, the hermeneutical question raised in chapter 1 remains: If Jesus' challenge to us is so central to the Christian message, how do we know what his challenge is, especially since we have Jesus' words and deeds only secondhand even in the Gospels? How if at all does one read between the lines of the biblical writings to find the person of Jesus who confronts and challenges, avoiding simply projecting a preconceived Jesus into the Bible? But before even a tentative answer to this question can be given, a second but closely related question must be explored: What is the relation of language, specifically Christian language, to a perceptual shift experience? Third, in calling for such growth is Jesus introducing something unique in history or is he expressing a recurrent theme in ancient Israel? Other questions include: Does the emphasis upon the Synoptic Gospels here not raise anew the question of a canon within the canon? And similarly, with the emphasis on Christian experience and criteria for its evaluation, is not the balance being shifted away from a Protestant *sola scriptura* to a more Catholic reliance upon the church (i.e., tradition) as the final authority for Christian faith? Or, more pointedly, wherein lies authority for Christian experience and theology? The list could grow much longer, for the sketch in this chapter has conclusively demonstrated nothing. If, however, it has intrigued the reader with the possible promise of an experiential theology based on existential phenomenology, it has been successful in its intent.

the re-creative power
of the word of god

C. DANIEL BATSON

In the preceding chapter Christian experience was characterized as involving a perceptual shift in response to Jesus' challenge, a more complex analogue of the figure-ground reversal
in Gestalt psychology. Now it is time to explore the psychodynamics of this process of Christian growth in more detail.
Processes of this sort have been given considerable attention by
psychologists studying creativity. Therefore, in this chapter we
shall first briefly review the psychological literature on creativity
in an attempt to better understand the internal dynamics of the
Christian perceptual shift. Once we have some understanding
of how this process occurs within an individual, the inquiry will
be extended to probe how it is possible to relate to the
perceptual shift process in the life of another, how the biblical
writer can affect our experience today. At this point we shall
focus on the role of religious language as a mediator for the
re-creation of religious experience. We shall find that it is not
enough to say that Christian language has creative power, that it
is a speech or word event. One must also probe the source of
this creative power. This source seems to lie not in some
ontological character of the language itself (as the new hermeneuticians suggest) but in the creative experience of the author
of that language, in the creative perceptual shift experience
it was coined to express and, potentially, to re-create in

the life of another. It is in the context of this experience-language-experience sequence that we speak of the re-creative power of the Word of God.

I
CREATIVE CHRISTIAN GROWTH:
THE PERCEPTUAL SHIFT

A
Classic Psychological Views of the Creative Process

Gestalt. Consonant with the outline of the perceptual shift in chapter 2, Gestalt psychologists point to the perceptual character of creative thought. They speak of the creative process as a perceptual restructuring, as "insight," "productive thinking," or the "ahah," and emphasize the shift in one's perceptual structures toward a "better" Gestalt, toward an easier way to think about one's experience—better form, organization, etc. The classic Gestalt statement on creativity is by Max Wertheimer in *Productive Thinking.* There he outlines the structural change process.

Thinking consists in envisaging, realizing structural features and structural requirement; proceeding in accordance with, and determined by, these requirements; thereby changing the situation in the direction of structural improvements, which involve: that gaps, trouble-regions, disturbances, superficialities be viewed and dealt with structurally . . . looking for structural rather than piecemeal truth.[1]

Gestalt analyses of creativity are, however, less explicit when it comes to the dynamics of the creative process itself. To emphasize the discontinuity between one's original perception (S_1) and the postinsight perception (S_2), Wertheimer models the transition process simply as $S_1 \ldots S_2$. The before and after states are recognized, but nothing is said about the change process itself.

Thus, the Gestalt analysis seems quite helpful in (1) identifying the phenomenon for consideration, changes in the structures with which we actively shape our experience, (2) identifying the motivations for such changes, "gaps, trouble-regions, disturbances, superficialities"—changes occur when inconsistencies and/or disfunctionalities appear in our existing structures, when our reality "no longer works"—and (3) suggesting the goal of the change process, toward an easier way to think. But Gestalt psychology is regrettably silent as to what the dynamics of the change process itself may be. The process itself is reduced to an ellipsis between the beginning and end states.

Psychoanalytic. The sequence of the process of creative thought has, however, been extensively discussed by psychoanalytic theorists. The psychoanalytic attention to unconscious and preconscious as well as conscious processes seems to allow for a probing of the dynamics of creative growth at greater depth than does the basically perceptual Gestalt model.

Freud himself tended to skirt the problem of creativity, feeling that it was not directly amenable to analytic research. He does, however, leave several clues as to his conception of the process, first, in his treatment of fantasy, dreams, and free association in the therapeutic process and, second, in discussions of sublimation as a key to understanding men of genius.[2] Much psychoanalytic theory about creativity since Freud has focused on the second of these clues, sublimation. In the creative person unconscious, libidinal impulses are not repressed by the ego but are deflected or sublimated into ego-acceptable channels of curiosity and investigation. Two aspects of the sublimation model deserve comment in the light of more recent developments in psychoanalytic theory: nonconscious participation in creativity and personal conflict as a motivator for it.

1. As the emphasis in analytic theory has shifted from unconscious id impulses to reality-oriented ego functions in neo-Freudian psychoanalytic theory, conceptions of the nature of nonconscious participation in the creative process have changed. For example, Ernst Kris introduces the concept of "ego regression," in which "the ego may use the primary process and not only be overwhelmed by it."[3] For Kris and other neo-Freudians the emphasis tends to be upon the "preconscious" as the mediational system between conscious and unconscious and thus on "regression in the service of the ego." Rather than the ego simply forcing deflection of the powerful libidinal impulses as Freud's sublimation model suggests, Kris contends that ego functions are intentionally relaxed in the creative act in order to gain access to unconscious processes.

Lawrence Kubie takes this logical progression from Freud's conception of an unconsciously driven creative process one step further, placing creativity squarely within the preconscious and viewing either conscious or unconscious domination of that process as neurotic distortions. The preconscious processes, having access to both conscious and unconscious but being driven by neither, have the capacity "to find new and unexpected connections, to voyage freely over the seas, . . . to find new relationships in time and space, and thus new meanings."[4]

2. The Freudian emphasis upon sublimation implies a second characteristic of the creative process, one which has not dropped from subsequent analytic conceptions. The motivator for creativity is personal conflict. In Freudian thought this is clearly expressed in viewing creativity as one form of resolution of the tension generated by inexpressible libidinal impulses. With the more recent emphasis upon the ego in psychoanalytic theory, Freud's particular formulation of the conflicts initiating the creative process is less emphasized, but it is still affirmed that problems generating creative growth are not simply academic questions but are, as Harold Rugg, for example, says, "felt-thought," issues in which the person is ego involved. This emphasis on ego-involving conflicts as the initiator of the creative thought seems to parallel the Gestalt emphasis on the breakdown of one's reality.

Post-Freudians such as Karen Horney, Erich Fromm, Carl Rogers, Abraham Maslow, and Rollo May have, however, added a significant element to the classical Freudian understanding of psychological conflict. Seeking to accent growth motivation as well as deficiency or defense motivation (Maslow's terms), the healthy personality as well as the pathological, these clinicians speak of the creative person as one who is not only capable of handling psychic conflict but even seeks novelty and uncertainty.[5] As was noted in chapter 2, the growth which Jesus sought to generate also seems to have this conflict- and ambiguity-seeking character.

Psychoanalytically based conceptions of creativity have been summarized in several stage models of the process. Although the best known of these models do not come from analytic theorists themselves, they show the clear mark of psychoanalytic interpretations of creative thought. Mathematician Henri Poincaré describes intuitive solutions to problems of theoretical mathematics (his discovery of Fuchsian functions) coming as a "sudden illumination" after having given up conscious work on the problem and allowing "unconscious work." He further insists that a subsequent period of conscious verification of the illumination is necessary, for the certainty which accompanies insight does not always prove justified. In a parallel analysis, Graham Wallas makes what has become the classic formulation of the stages in the creative process in *The Art of Thought*.[6] Wallas labels four stages: (1) preparation—the problem is examined and researched from all angles; (2) incubation—the individual gives up conscious thought on the problem; (3) illumination—the "happy idea" occurs (also included in this stage is consideration of the psychological factors that immediately precede and accompany illumination, such as increased emotional tension); and (4) verification—the validity of the idea is tested and it is refined to exact form. Both of these sequences reflect the psychoanalytic emphasis on the role of the off-conscious mind (unconscious or preconscious) in creativity and initiation of the process by ego-involving conflicts. Finally, both emphasize the ability of the creative individual to engage positively the tension and effort which accompany such conflicts.

The psychoanalytically oriented theorist who has perhaps most clearly extended such an analysis of creativity to apply to religious experience is Harold Rugg. Conducting a wide-ranging descriptive analysis of examples of creative thought in his posthumous *Imagination,* Rugg delineates a sequence of stages in the process of creative imagination quite similar to those of Poincaré and Wallas.

There is *first* a long, *conscious* preparatory period of baffled struggle; *second,* an interlude in which the scientist or artist apparently gives up, pushes the problem back or down or "out of mind," leaving it for the nonconscious to work upon. Then, *third,* comes the blinding and unexpected "flash of insight," and it comes with such certitude that a logical statement of it can be immediately prepared. These stages are present whether in art, science, technology, or philosophy.[7]

This "flash of insight" occurs, says Rugg, in the "transliminal mind," a "threshold antechamber" between the conscious mind and the unconscious having access to both and a greater autistic freedom than either. Rugg notes that this process seems to characterize mystical and religious experiences, the tao of the East and of the West. The parallel of the transliminal to Kubie's preconscious should be apparent.

To conclude, these psychoanalytically based conceptions of creativity do seem to carry one deeper into the dynamics of the process itself than do the Gestalt theories, but they also have a major limitation. Although they outline a sequence of stages in the process, they give little explanatory clarity as to the why of this sequence, other than to say that it is necessary for the unconscious or preconscious to work. It is very difficult to put one's finger on (i.e., to operationalize) precisely what is meant by "psychic conflict," and it is even more difficult to specify what "incubation," "illumination," "imagination," "unconscious," "preconscious," or "transliminal mind" mean and how they interact. Critical elements in the creative sequence have been named, and their theoretical function has even been described in a general way. But any clear and precise explanation of the dynamics of the process, the factors which shape its character, seems lacking. Because of this vagueness many psychologists would agree with J.P. Guilford in his 1950 presidential address to the American Psychological Association that, rather than assisting in our understanding of the creative process, these terms actually cloak it in an unnecessarily impenetrable mystery. The qualitative difference between our conscious and our unconscious and preconscious processes as the concepts are developed in analytic theory makes it difficult if not impossible to explain a process grounded in the latter.

B
A Contemporary Psychological Model of Creativity

More recently in psychology, information-processing theorists, working from a computer analogy and conducting experimental research, have attempted to develop an understanding of creativity which takes account of insights from both Gestalt and psychoanalytic theory and shows promise for overcoming the weaknesses of each.[8] First, with the Gestalt psychologists they emphasize perceptual structures with which one creates himself and his world, viewing the creative process as involving changes in these structures toward a more complex, open, and better integrated reality. Second, they also provide a model for understanding the dynamics of this process, as do the analytic theorists, but without being forced to speak of "unconscious" or "preconscious" processes. The off-conscious mind which is central to analytic theories may be viewed in information-processing terms as the perceptual structures themselves. As existential phenomenologist Maurice Merleau-Ponty says, these are "invisible" structures, the schema which we use to make sense of our experience, the framework on which our very reality is woven. These structures are to be carefully distinguished from the information one processes through the structures. The perceptual structures provide the framework requisite for logic, language, and, therefore, for consciousness as traditionally defined. Therefore, a change of the structures themselves (creativity) is necessarily nonlogical, nonlinguistic, and nonconscious.[9]

Concerning the impetus and result of the creative process, as Gestaltists suggest, such changes are motivated by some failure in one's existing structures; "cracks" or gaps appear in one's reality (or, in the psychoanalytic framework, an ego-involving conflict arises). The result is a new structural organization, a new reality which allows one to process more information coming from his environment more effectively. This creative restructuring should not be considered simply a solution to a given problem. Restructuring does not solve a problem or resolve a conflict, for solutions require closure and necessarily occur in the context of a given structural set. Rather, restructuring puts the conflictual elements together in a new way—a new reality is born.[10] And the criteria for evaluation of a reality cannot be logical but must be functional; at issue is what one's reality enables him to do, not whether it is "true."

Creative restructuring is an internal operation necessary and even possible only when the active use of the present perceptual structures breaks down, when either because of internal contradictions or new experiences the present reality ceases to function (cf. Wallas' incubation stage and Rugg's interlude).

Using the computer analogy, reprograming is necessary only when the existing program cannot process the input information. If creative, the restructuring not only allows one's reality to function again but to incorporate a wider range of experience; a new and "larger" world has been created for the individual. But as Poincaré and Wallas suggest, if this new world is to be other than a fantasy world it must be verified or lived out in experience in one's social world. It demands expression in behavior.

If one were to present a stage sequence of the creative process paralleling those of Wallas and Rugg on the basis of these general principles derived from an information-processing perspective, it might be as follows: (1) stemming either from internal contradictions or encounter with new experiences, ego-involving *conflicts* or cracks appear in one's present perceptual structures; (2) after considerable effort, attempts to resolve the conflicts in the context of the existing structures are abandoned in *exhaustion;* (3) a *perceptual shift* occurs as the structures are re-formed in response to the functional breakdown; (4) the shift creates a new perceptual set and thereby a *new reality;* and (5) the new reality is *expressed* and *tested* in life in the social world. As one lives out his new reality, new conflicts or cracks will appear and the process begins again.[11]

C
Religious Creativity

At this point it may be helpful to consider several concrete examples of religious growth. These examples are by no means definitive or prescriptive, only illustrative. They have been selected primarily to display the range of contexts and contents possible for perceptual shifts in response to religious conflicts. No attempt will be made to evaluate the Christian creativity of these experiences in terms of increased awareness of and concern for others. For some, the necessary follow-up data are lacking; for others, the subsequent life is well known and the reader can judge for himself.

First, of course, there is the experience of Paul described in Acts 9 on the Damascus road in which his perception of himself in relation to the Jewish law and to Jesus is radically altered. Paul's experience requires little comment here; it is given far more attention in chapter 6. It is sufficient to note that a conflict between personal sin and divine justice is subsequently restructured in terms of faith and grace.

William James presents numerous examples of more contemporary religious experience in his classic *Varieties of Religious Experience.* Three will be sketched. Thoreau describes the following experience resulting from his chosen solitude:

Once, a few weeks after I came to the woods, for an hour I doubted whether the near neighborhood of man was not essential to a serene and healthy life. To be alone was somewhat unpleasant. But, in the midst of a gentle rain, while these thoughts prevailed, I was suddenly sensible of such sweet and beneficent society in nature, in the very pattering of the drops, and in every sight and sound around my house, an infinite and unaccountable friendliness all at once, like an atmosphere, sustaining me, as made the fancied advantages of human neighborhood insignificant, and I have never thought of them since. Every little pine-needle expanded and swelled with sympathy and befriended me. I was so distinctly made aware of the presence of something kindred to me, that I thought no place could ever be strange to me again.[12]

Quite different in context and content but similar in the emergence of a new perceived reality is the revival experience of an unnamed man:

I know not how I got back into the encampment, but found myself staggering up to Rev.———'s Holiness tent—and as it was full of seekers and a terrible noise inside, some groaning, some laughing, and some shouting, and by a large oak, ten feet from the tent, I fell on my face by a bench, and tried to pray, and every time I would call on God, something like a man's hand would strangle me by choking. I don't know whether there were any one around or near me or not. I thought I should surely die if I did not get help, but just as often as I would pray, that unseen hand was felt on my throat and my breath squeezed off. Finally something said: "Venture on the atonement, for you will die anyway if you don't." So I made one final struggle to call on God for mercy, with the same choking and strangling, determined to finish the sentence of prayer for mercy, if I did strangle and die, and the last I remember that time was falling back on the ground with the same unseen hand on my throat. I don't know how long I lay there or what was going on. None of my folks were present. When I came to myself, there were a crowd around me praising God. The very heavens seemed to open and pour down rays of light and glory. Not for a moment only, but all day and night, floods of light and glory seemed to pour through my soul, and oh, how I was changed, and everything became new. My horses and hogs and even everybody seemed changed.[13]

The following are excerpts from a description of one of his experiences by David Brainerd, whom James calls "that genuine saint."

One morning, while I was walking in a solitary place as usual, I at once saw that all my contrivances and projects to effect or procure deliverance and salvation for myself were utterly in vain; I was brought quite to a stand, as finding myself totally lost. I saw that it was forever impossible for me to do anything towards helping or delivering myself, that I had made all the pleas I ever could have made to all eternity; and that all my pleas were vain, for I saw that self-interest had led me to pray, and that I had never once prayed from any respect to the glory of God. . . .

I continued, as I remember, in this state of mind, from Friday morning till the Sabbath evening following (July 12, 1739), when I was walking again in the same solitary place. Here, in a mournful melancholy state *I was attempting to pray; but found no heart to engage in that or any other duty; my former concern, exercise, and religious affections were now gone. I thought that the Spirit of God had quite left me; but still was not distressed; yet disconsolate, as if there was nothing in heaven or earth could make me happy. Having been thus endeavoring to pray—though, as I thought, very stupid and senseless—*for near half an hour; then, as I was walking in a thick grove, unspeakable glory seemed to open to the apprehension of my soul. I do not mean any external brightness, nor any imagination of a body of light, but it was a new inward apprehension or view that I had of God, such as I never had before, nor anything which had the least resemblance to it. I had no particular apprehension of any one person in the Trinity, either the Father, the Son, or the Holy Ghost; but it appeared to be Divine glory. . . . My soul was so captivated and delighted with the excellency of God that I was even swallowed up in him; at least to that degree that I had no thought about my own salvation, and scarce reflected that there was such a creature as myself. I continued in this state of inward joy, peace, and astonishing, till near dark without any sensible abatement; and then began to think and examine what I had seen; and felt sweetly composed in my mind all the evening following. I felt myself in a new world, and everything about me appeared with a different aspect from what it was wont to do.[14]

Finally, here is a brief selection from the experience of a psychologist (S) in his late thirties under the influence of LSD reported by R.E.L. Masters and Jean Houston in *The Varieties of Psychedelic Experience.* Well into the session S summarizes the conflict:

All of my life I have been trying to cut loose from something at the bottom of myself that prevented me from going where I wanted to go and also from knowing what I wanted to know. What I wanted to know was, essentially, God. But before I could get to know God I had to cut loose from most of what bound me to the Devil. I am sorry that what I have learned cannot be put into terms that would seem to be more scientific. I continue to have some resistance to understanding myself in these terms of God and Devil, Heaven and Hell, although I believe that these terms are the only ones really acceptable to me and effective as instruments of change.[15]

Then, under the direction of the guide (G) and in response to imagery produced by concentration on a little porcelain mermaid:

G: "You have mentioned many times your 'evil roots,' those roots going down to the place you feel that you came from. Do you still feel those roots now?"
S: "My roots extended down to that other place. I have had to cut myself away from my roots one by one. I have a sense now of having cut through so many of these roots that there may not be too many of them left."
G: "Good, then maybe now you can pull free. Try pulling free. *Pull free now!*"
S (Waves his feet in the air, makes jerking motions with his feet and legs, etc.): "I feel like I really am free! But it was so easy! I broke them off where they came into the soles of my feet. They were dry as dust and just crumbled when I started to pull away from them. Like dried old umbilicals, attached to the bottoms of my feet, and I've broken them all off. Why didn't I know before that they were ready to crumble? How long could they have been like that? Why, now I am free!" S was smiling, very excited and looked extremely pleased and happy.
G: "And this hold that you say the Devil has had on you? What about that?"
S: "Satan has no more power to control me! I still have habit to fear, but the organic link is gone! What I just kicked loose was the whole serpent identification and the dead crumbling umbilical cord that still was tying me down to Hell. I seem to have shattered every physical connection with the place below. Look! (S gets up and stamps his feet against the ground.) I am crumbling the last remnants of the connection under my feet. I shake off the last of the dust and I step free of it all. My perception with regard to matter was what triggered everything off—seeing in the

face of the little mermaid that it could be shaped in so many ways according to the way I looked at it. Intellectually, of course, I was aware of this before. But now I really knew it to be so and it seemed that from there I could go on to other real knowledge."

S now walked around the room, picking up his feet, shaking them, and declaring he was freeing himself from the last remnants of the "dust" that linked him to the "down below" aspects of his past. He looked at us, smiled very happily, and said: "It is over." The session had lasted less than five hours and the drug effects were cut off about as abruptly as lights go off when someone flips the switch.[16]

Reflecting on this experience later, S felt that "a destructive response to the world has been replaced by a response that is essentially creative."[17]

In each example the person has been struggling with an ego-involving conflict of religious scope which has shattered at least some portion of his reality. Despairing, he suddenly finds himself in a new world, one in which the elements of this conflict are seen anew so that the conflict no longer has a stranglehold on him. It should be noted that these conflicts, as with other religious conflicts (for example, the meaning of life given death), are not amenable to "solution" within a given reality. They are irresolvable, lacking right answers. Whether or not one's response to such conflicts is creative depends on the direction in which the new reality moves the individual. Does the new reality test out, allowing the person to encounter more of his experience more responsibly? For the particular examples cited, insufficient data force us to reserve any final judgments.

II
RE-CREATIVE
CHRISTIAN GROWTH

With a clearer grasp of the dynamics of Christian growth within the individual, attention may be turned to the interpersonal process of influencing this growth process in another person's life. The question is far from easy. Not only does the perceptual shift necessarily occur deep within an individual, he cannot even consciously control it. It often appears to be bestowed from outside, to overpower him. How then can one person relate to this process in another? Or, more pointedly, how can Jesus' challenge creatively affect the religious growth of an individual today? Even if, as Kierkegaard claims, the Bible allows us to have as direct access to Jesus as did his contemporaries, the question still remains. How was Jesus able to affect the reality of his contemporaries? And to the degree that one moves away from Kierkegaard's extremely optimistic hermeneutic and acknowledges that the biblical record is not simply transparent, especially across a two-thousand-year generation gap, the problem only becomes compounded. Then one must also deal with the intermediating role of the biblical writer and his language.

There are thus three stages in re-creative Christian growth: the creative encounter with Jesus which the biblical writer is attempting to express, the language of the Bible, and men today seeking to deal with religious conflicts creatively. Since Jesus confronted his contemporary in a social and linguistic context, the experience of the biblical writer is also that of a man seeking to deal with religious conflicts, i.e., there is a recurring cycle with parallel dynamics. For the present analysis the focus will be on the more accessible and immediately relevant stage, the re-creation in a modern man of the experience of which the biblical writer spoke. But the results of this analysis would seem to suggest clues for probing interaction between Jesus and his contemporary as well.

The Christian re-creative process begins and ends in the experience of individuals, but it is mediated by language. In the preceding section consideration was given to the creative process within the individual; at this point attention must be turned to an analysis of the character of Christian language which allows it to serve this mediating function and how it may be "rightly handled" or interpreted so that a link may be made between the experience which generated the language and the experience of the hearer.

A
Potentially Creative Symbolic Language

The thesis is that the Christian language system, to the extent that it is perceived as being the "word of God," emerged out of and is concerned with the generation in others of creative Christian growth. This re-creative function seems possible because central to Christian language (but not unique to it) is a particular type of language, potentially creative symbolic language. It is necessary to outline the structural characteristics of this type of language to provide a context for considering its functional dynamic in Christian re-creation.[18]

1. *Structural characteristics of potentially creative symbolic language.* Symbol and symbolic are used here in a specific and technical sense relating to three linguistic dialectics—semantic, analogic, and synthetic—in at least two of which any potentially creative symbolic expression must necessarily participate.

a. *Semantic.* The first dialectic leads to meaning and is basic to the existence of any language at all. Since symbolic language as the term is used here is a specific type of language, it quite naturally follows that the semantic dialectic is a necessary but not sufficient foundation for symbolic language. In briefest terms, the tension involved in the semantic dialectic is that between the world of experience and the world of language and concepts. One must conceptually "turn his back on" the particular experience before him to be able to develop and use language to speak of that experience. To use the term "tree," for example, to refer to a given phenomenon, one must turn his back on the immediate perception and relate it to the conceptual generalization "tree." As Susanne Langer notes, the "conceptual" use of speech is "originally impractical." The phenomena immediately present must be turned from (in dialectical language, negated) in order that a linguistic referent relating to the phenomena may be affirmed (synthesis).[19]

b. *Analogic.* The semantic dialectic brings one to the level of language; the second dialectic, the analogic, brings one to the symbolic, a subcategory within language. The analogic dialectic involves the negation of the ordinary use of a word or phrase so that it may be "freed" for use in an unusual way within a specific language system. Fundamental to this process is Wittgenstein's now well-known notion of "language games." Various angles for viewing experience lead to differing languages, both with regard to how a given word is used and the grammars for uniting these words. The dialectical nature of this process may be accented by considering the religious phrase "heavenly father." What the phrase seems to suggest is: God is like a father (positive analogy); God is not like any father you have ever known (negative analogy); God is a heavenly father (odd synthesis accenting intimacy and yet otherness and mystery).

This dialectic has been aptly characterized as the "maraschino cherry" process.[20] Apparently in making maraschino cherries all the original coloring is first bleached out of the cherry before the new "super red" coloring is added. This illustration is particularly appropriate because the form of the cherry remains the same, but the cherry is unusual or odd in its coloring and taste and used in specific situations where ordinary cherries would be inappropriate. The process of symbolization seems to refer to this crossing of linguistic boundaries upon which the analogic dialectic is based (of course, the language need not be verbal, as for example in art and music).

c. *Synthetic.* It is the third dialectic which holds the key to potentially creative symbolic language, the language which is directed toward generation within another of one's creative experience. The synthesis of which this dialectic is an expression is that reached intrapersonally in the process of creative growth. That is, when a person begins to test a new reality in the social world, he seeks to express the character of the change which has taken place. Because it is a change in the perceptual structures themselves upon which language is based, it cannot be captured in language. Rather, language is used in an odd symbolic way in an attempt to evoke an understanding of and perhaps participation in the experienced change.

The oddity of this symbolization is not the same as that of the analogic dialectic, although it is related. The analogic dialectic involves negation of the ordinary meaning of a linguistic element so that it can carry a new specialized meaning in order to describe some aspect of one's social world from a particular perspective. In contrast, the synthetic dialectic attempts to evoke understanding of a lived experience which transcends the social and linguistic world. Thus, one often finds that it involves the use of mysterious and "ultimate" symbols. In addition to religious symbols such as God, Christ, or Love, examples which have recently emerged in the United States include: "I have a dream," "black power," and even "law and order." These phrases are used not so much to convey information as to evoke understanding of a new reality, participation in it, and consequent response. When such symbols arise they naturally tend to be collected into a special language system, odd in the analogic sense. Further, a special sense of community emerges among those who use the language. Thus, a given linguistic term or phrase may participate in both the analogic and synthetic dialectics simultaneously, but the two functions are quite different and so the maintenance of the distinction between them seems necessary.

The dialectic tension in the mysterious and ultimate symbolic language which participates in the synthetic dialectic is that contained in the ego-involving conflicts or cracks in one's perceptual structures. If the shift to a new reality is creative, it restructures the conflicting elements synthetically. Thus, *the synthesis involved in the synthetic dialectic is that of the perceptual shift itself expressed linguistically.* It is because of this origin in creative growth that such language has creative potential. This observation will be foundational to consideration of the functional dynamics of re-creative language.

With its dialectical character outlined, specific forms of potentially creative symbolic language may be noted. Such language seems to find expression in at least six general forms: myth, saga, rite, story, parable, and a particular type of symbol. Numerous examples of the various forms of potentially creative symbolic language are presented in Part Three, especially chapter 4, so the present discussion will be very brief.

In religious language, the first three of these forms—myth, saga, and rite—tend to be most dominant in ancient cultures, though examples of each may, of course, be found in any "modern" culture. With regard to myth, Susanne Langer notes:

Myth, at least at its best, is a recognition of natural conflicts, of human desire frustrated by nonhuman powers, hostile oppression, or contrary desires; it is a story of the birth, passion and defeat by death which is man's common fate. Its ultimate end is not wishful distortion of the world, but serious envisagement of its fundamental truths, moral orientation, not escape.[21]

Thus, the creative potential in myth lies in the fact that it presents in narrative form the symbolization of conflicts which are experienced by a sizable percentage of the culture. The limitation of myth and saga (the dynamics of which seem similar to myth), however, lies in their strong cultural mooring; they tend to express creative restructuring in culture-specific forms.

Similarly, the potentially creative aspect of rite is to be found in the symbolic acting out of the experiences depicted in a myth or saga. Thus, for example, upon coming of age in some cultures, the male child is brought forth through the legs of the tribesmen, being "born" into adulthood, the culture's creative handling of the conflict between a quite distinct classification of child and adult and the gradual developmental process.

In world religions, potentially creative symbolic language also finds expression in stories, parables, and "dialectical symbols."[22] Briefly stated, stories and parables seem to operate as transcultural myths. Like myths, stories and parables seem geared to a specific conflict and to presenting in narrative form a symbolic restructuring of this conflict. But, unlike myths, neither the conflict nor the restructuring is couched in culture-specific symbols. Illustrative of this point is the parable of the good Samaritan. It expresses and challenges restructuring of one's relation to his neighbor, a relationship which is common cross-culturally. And the relevance of the parable to many cultural settings is readily apparent. Story and parable seem to be the dominant forms of potentially creative symbolic language which Jesus used in presenting his challenge to creative growth.

Dialectical symbols are those transcultural symbols (verbally, usually a phrase; in art, a given painting or sculpture) into which the restructuring of one's reality through a perceptual shift has been kernelized. The dialectic referred to is the synthetic dialectic in which one's reality is restructured creatively. Often, rather than emerging in narrative form in a story or parable, the expression leads to the creation of a new term or phrase or the reinterpretation of an old one so that it summarizes the impact of the entire creative experience. Thus, the dialectical symbol is a capsulized linguistic expression of individual creative growth.

The paradigm example of a dialectical symbol (and indeed the context in which the term originated) is Kierkegaard's "God-man." For Kierkegaard this symbol emerges from a restructuring of the attempt of man in his finitude to reach the infinite. In the

Moment of absolute frustration and exhaustion of reason, the "God-man" is bestowed. The impossible struggle of man to reach God is seen anew; the infinite has become finite in the incarnation; God and man are linked in Jesus Christ. The "God-man" symbol kernelizes this liberating insight.[23]

2. *Functional dynamics of potentially creative symbolic language.* With the foregoing outline of the structure of potentially creative symbolic language as a conceptual backdrop, attention may now be turned to the critical question of how such language functions in stimulation of another's creative Christian growth. Again, the thesis is that potentially creative symbolic language emerges from an author's attempt to express and evoke an experience of creative growth and thereby has the potential for re-creating such an experience.[24] The first pole of this thesis, the grounding of potentially creative symbolic language in the personal creative experience of its author, has already been emphasized; such language is an expression in one's social world of the perceptual shift. The second pole, the power of such language to re-create creative growth paralleling that out of which it emerged, remains to be discussed.

Ian Ramsey's phrases, "the penny drops" and "the light dawns," point the way for a functional analysis of this re-creative power of potentially creative symbolic language but are unable to take us any distance down the road. Considering a story which depicts God as "Unity," he notes:

The story must be told and continue to be told until there breaks in on us at some point a situation characteristically different from its predecessors; until at some point or other the penny drops, the light dawns, there is a characteristic "disclosure" and there is evolved that situation in relation to which the word "unite" is to be commended.[25]

The basic functional question is: How does the symbolic language actually evoke the situation? What characteristics of this type of language make this possible? Regrettably, here Ramsey is unable to shed any light, fleeing these questions as inappropriate and smacking of psychological reductionism. Yet surely the penny drops not just because one repeats the story over and over again but because with a variation in emphasis the story suddenly strikes deeper than conceptual understanding.

What is the nature of this variation in emphasis? Returning to the synthetic dialectic as integral to potentially creative symbolic language, one remembers that packed within such language are both the conflictual aspects of the prior reality and their synthetic restructuring which the perceptual shift provides. *What seems to be required to allow such a symbol to "live" for someone else is that these conflictual and synthetic elements be "unpacked." This unpacking is a dual-pronged process. It involves (a) sharpening of conflict and (b) providing a matrix for expression.* Whether it occurs implicitly or explicitly, this process seems necessary to enable the language to function as a vehicle relating one person's experience of creative growth to the lived experience of another.

Before considering each element of the process, it is extremely important to recognize that the unpacking hypothesis suggests that one is able to influence another's creative growth only at its end points, the conflict and expression stages, for it is only at these points that the intrapersonal process touches the sociocultural linguistic world. Whether another engages a conflict creatively and experiences a perceptual shift is out of the speaker's immediate control.[26] Thus the present analysis suggests it is impossible to force another's creative growth, but that a context may be provided which is more or less optimal for the evoking of such experiences, optimal being approached through the use of potentially creative symbolic language which may be unpacked so that conflicts are sharpened and a matrix of expression is provided. "He that has ears, let him hear."

a. *The sharpening of conflict.* If the potentially creative symbolic language expresses creative restructuring of a conflict which is existential for the hearer, then the language may function to allow the hearer to articulate and experience this conflict more directly. Absolutely vital to this sharpening process is that it be a conflict already existent in the hearer's reality structure, at least in nascent form. The role of one who enables creative growth is not to engender or create conflicts. Rather, the sharpening process involves bringing into awareness conflicts and tensions already existent in the other's perceptual set, but of which he may be either unaware or trying to ignore. If the conflict expressed in the potentially creative symbolic language does not relate to a conflict present in another's reality, to force the language on him cannot stimulate his creative process but will only produce a misunderstanding of the language.[27]

b. *The matrix of expression.* A matrix of expression may be provided by the synthetic kernel of the potentially creative symbolic language. This synthetic kernel must not, however, be treated as an answer or solution to the conflict. To do so would result in appropriation of the message entirely within the present structures and would reduce the process to propagation of an ideology. Rather, potentially creative symbolic language functions as a matrix of expression by providing the hearer with a linguistic system developed by others to speak about their experiences of growth with regard to a given conflict. In this way he is provided with a functionally valuable language to express his own experience in the social world.

As an example of the unpacking process, Kierkegaard's use of "God-man" again serves as prototypic. Most of his writings, especially the *Philosophical Fragments,* are an unpacking of this basic symbol. Within his latently Hegelian framework, Kierkegaard experiences the conflict to which the "God-man" speaks both philosophically (subject versus object or finite versus infinite) and theologically (impending death versus the eternal God). Kierkegaard also finds in the "God-man" a clue to a matrix of expression for the restructuring of this conflict, the biblical language which speaks of the Incarnate Christ.

Let us summarize this sketch of the structure and function of potentially creative symbolic language. Such language is the form in which the creative experience of the speaker enters the social world. It is characterized by three dialectical structures. The semantic dialectic it shares with all language, the analogic with all symbolic language, but the synthetic dialectic is unique to this particular kind of language. In various historical and cultural contexts potentially creative symbolic language appears in different forms: myth, saga, rite, story, parable, and dialectical symbols. These forms vary in their generality but each contains the elements of an existential conflict restructured synthetically into a new perception. Because of this structural character, this type of symbolic language has the potential of being unpacked by the hearer, perhaps through the aid of an interpreter, so that parallel existential conflicts in his life are sharpened and he is provided with a linguistic matrix for expressing his own perceptual shift in response to these conflicts. In this way potentially creative symbolic language mediates the re-creation of one individual's creative experience in the life of another. This skeletal model of the re-creation process will be fleshed out with concrete examples in the next chapter.

B
Christian Re-creation

Given this general model of the way language can function as mediator of creative growth, its implications for re-creative Christian growth must be noted. The model suggests the immense potential importance of both Christian language and Christian tradition, *but* (an extremely important *but*) not because of any qualities intrinsic to either per se. Rather, such language has potential importance because it has emerged from various individuals' creative encounter with existential religious concerns such as the meaning of life (and death) and how we are to relate to our fellowman. The potential value of the Christian tradition is in its ability, rightly handled, to provide an interpretive context to aid in unpacking the language of the Bible so that we may experience a perceptual restructuring with regard to existential religious questions.

This rather Bultmannian emphasis cannot be allowed to stand alone, however. It must also be emphasized that such language was not simply handed down from on high; it has emerged as a specific language system (cf. analogic dialectic) because it has creative potential (synthetic dialectic). Thus, the Bible has re-creative power for today, it is experienced as the Word of God, to the extent that its language expresses creative handling of conflicts which are existential for man today. Building upon this premise, the task of the reader of the Bible is to unpack its potentially creative symbolic language, allowing it to "live"— live not in the sense that Jesus seems real or alive but in the sense that one lives the conflict (if, in fact, it is his conflict) and has the opportunity for creative restructuring paralleling that which the biblical writer experienced in response to Jesus' challenge. The language provides a context for the reader's re-creation. In this re-creative process Christian language is experienced as the Word of God.

III
HERMENEUTICAL GUIDELINES

Reflecting upon this analysis of re-creative Christian growth, two hermeneutical observations must be made. First, before one can say anything positive about the meaning and function of Christian, especially biblical, language for modern man, he should preface his attempt with a "negative hermeneutic" which asks critically whether such language is even relevant. On the basis of our model for re-creative growth, it becomes clear that someone's potentially creative symbolic language is relevant for me only to the degree that the existential conflicts with which he is wrestling overlap with those impinging on me. If not, the language may be potentially creative for someone else but not for me.

Obviously, many of the conflicts which the biblical writer faced do not face us, and many of our concerns are totally foreign to him. Does this mean the Bible is simply irrelevant to one's religious life today? It is difficult to say. What can be said is that, if the foregoing analysis is correct, the creative aspects of the biblical message are not its comments on the political situation of the day or even the world view which it reflects (though each of these is worthy of study). The Bible's value lies in its expression of man's creative encounter with basic religious and ethical questions such as: Given the imminence of my death, what is the meaning of life? Or: How shall I relate to my fellowman? Questions like these seem as alive today as they have been for thousands of years. Thus, there would seem to be some rather basic points of contact between our experience and that of the biblical writer.[28]

But certainly the social and cultural context in which one asks these questions does much to shape their character. As one's reality becomes more remote to a given world view, the relevance of the experience of and expression about such religious concerns of those living in that world view to his experience would seem more remote, for they would not be living with the same reality. Since existential conflicts, the motivator for religious experience, come as irresolvable gaps or cracks in one's reality, existential conflicts would differ to the degree that realities differ. In one sense, we share the same religious questions as the biblical writer, for we are faced with problems such as death and our relations with others as certainly as was he. But in another sense the questions differ, for they are shaped by one's sociocultural context and world view. We thus come again to what would seem to be the central question for the negative hermeneutic, one with which Bultmann continually wrestled: To what degree do we share the existential religious conflicts which the biblical writer experienced?

Although this question defies any simple answer, the "Conflict Cones" model that follows suggests one way to conceive the overlap of conflicts for different individuals. The model implies that each human individual has certain totally idiosyncratic conflicts or concerns, because we each have a uniquely personal reality. There are other conflicts, however, which he shares with an increasingly broad sociocultural context, from primary group through subculture and culture up to a civilization level and perhaps beyond. The most general level seems to be that of existential religious conflicts, such as those already noted, being common to all men, at least in a given civilization. Questions generated by a given religion, however (e.g., How do I respond to Jesus' challenge?), are less generally shared.

The experience and creative expression of another is relevant for one's own creative growth according to the degree of overlap of their two conflict cones at the level in question. Thus, for example, individuals A and B do not share either idiosyncratic or primary group reality and conflicts. They do, however, participate in overlapping subcultures, and from here up to the level of general existential conflicts the experience and expression of one will be increasingly relevant to the other. B and C, however, share some overlap from the primary group up. If two individuals' cones do not overlap at a given level, direct empathy between them does not exist and the creative symbolic language of one will not be directly creative for the other. One

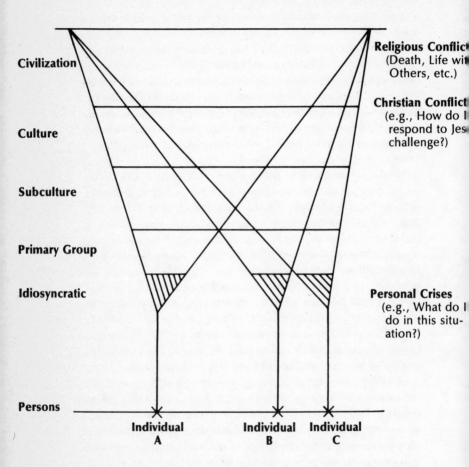

Civilization

Religious Conflict
(Death, Life with
Others, etc.)

Christian Conflict
(e.g., How do I
respond to Jesus
challenge?)

Culture

Subculture

Primary Group

Idiosyncratic

Personal Crises
(e.g., What do I
do in this situ-
ation?)

Persons

Individual
A

Individual
B

Individual
C

CONFLICT CONES

is then limited to an analogic understanding of another's reality and conflicts, a relationship which seems to require reinterpretation of the other's language (i.e., symbolic translation) before it can function creatively.

The various levels are not, of course, intended to be mutually exclusive; one's reality includes all levels, as do his conflicts, although conflictual pressure may focus at a given level at a given time (e.g., at the cultural level when the Pentagon papers were released and the issue of national security versus an informed electorate became focal). Thus, to look for "exclusively" religious conflicts is misleading; rather, at certain points the conflict pattern pushes one back to a religious level of basic reexamination of the core of his reality.

The funnel shape of the cones implies broad generality of religious experience and language across cultures and perhaps even civilizations. This claim seems to receive at least partial support from the immense diversity of age and cultural origin of the religious writings at popular book stands—Eastern as well as Western, ancient as well as modern. Certainly it is not matched by any other area. But to claim broadest generality does not end the issue. The key question remains: Has our conflict cone generally ceased to intersect with that of the biblical writers, even at this general level? This question is pursued further in chapter 6.

Second and more briefly, the re-creative growth model suggests that no positive hermeneutic can concentrate on the meaning of the language alone or even the experience-generating power of the language without also giving attention to the experience out of which the language emerged. The three levels of (1) creative experience (in this case that of the biblical writer), (2) language, and (3) re-creative experience (contemporary man) must all be considered as a communicative unit. This observation is made as a corrective to the New Hermeneutic analysis of the Word and its re-creative power. Advocates of the New Hermeneutic analyze this re-creative aspect of the experience-language interaction without giving adequate consideration to the source of this potentially creative Word. Such narrowness seems to force these writers into increasingly grand ontological assertions in an attempt to explain the dynamic power of the Word, a power it has been suggested lies in its source in the creative experience of the author in response to the life and ministry of Jesus. It can re-create Christian growth because it expresses creative Christian growth.

To summarize this chapter a recap seems in order. Drawing heavily from psychological and philosophical insights we have attempted to explore the dynamics of the experience-language-experience process of re-creation of Christian experience in the life of another. First, the experience itself, represented in the two end points of this process, was examined through an analysis of its creative character. Then attention was turned to the missing link, the particular kind of language capable of mediating between the creative perceptual shift experience in one life and in another. It was suggested that potentially creative symbolic language has the power to serve as a catalyst for creative growth because it is itself the linguistic expression of such growth and carries within it creative insight. Therefore, the potentially creative symbolic language of the Bible may serve as the catalyst for creative Christian growth today because it expresses the perceptual-shift experience of the biblical writer. In this way Jesus' challenge may be mediated to modern man.

These observations suggested both negative and positive hermeneutical guidelines. Negatively, unless we share the existential religious conflicts which faced the biblical writer, and it is difficult to say to what degree we do, his words have lost creative power for us. Positively, the experiential origin of biblical language is an essential aspect of any Christian hermeneutic. Without a focus on this origin, one is forced to ontologize the language itself in an attempt to explain its power. The Bible is not the Word of God because of any quality intrinsic to it. Rather, it is experienced as the Word of God because of its power to guide man's growth in response to religious existential conflicts. And it has this power because it expresses precisely a growth process. To further support this thesis a careful look must be taken at the actual language of the Bible. This is done for both the Old and New Testaments in Part Three.

The Bible and Christian Experience

religious experience and language in the old testament

W. MALCOLM CLARK

Purists who say that only categories intrinsic to the conscious viewpoints of the participants in a culture are adequate to the analysis of the culture will find the approach here inadequate. Such a position would, for example, exclude all anthropological study of primitive society which brings concepts to the analysis and detects models operating in the society which are neither conscious in the minds of the members of the society nor simply imposed by the investigator. Two questions which provide the rationale for the presence of this and the following chapter in this joint investigation of experiential theology as well as much of the stimulus leading to such new insights as may appear are: (1) Does an experiential theology suggest, in the way of a changed perspective in studying the Old Testament, that we look for something different, concentrate on different data, or look at old problems from a different viewpoint? (2) What may we find in the Old Testament which may confirm, modify, or deny the thrust of experiential theology as discussed in the other chapters? It will often be impossible or unfruitful to address ourselves explicitly to these two questions at each stage of the argument and even more so to try to decide which conclusions are the fruit of an approach influenced by experiential theology, which conclusions independently confirm similar conclusions reached elsewhere in this book, and which conclusions themselves provided data which was significant in the evolution of our understanding of experiential theology. If the material is to have integrity, it must follow its own intrinsic development. Even to ask these two questions may lead to distortion resulting from the lack of a balanced picture. Such balance will have to wait for future development of the inquiry which, one hopes, will be able to utilize creatively some of the reaction to the initial outline presented here. Admittedly some broad general assertions approach the status of trial balloons, while others call out for detailed argumentation in technical journal articles. Indeed, some of the things which will be said are more a way of looking at the material than factual assertions and may not be fully subject to validity tests. In this chapter, I will take up the theme of the perceptual shift as we look at religious experience in the Old Testament and at the relation of language to experience. The next chapter will concentrate on a debunking thrust and a related openness to experience manifested in ancient Israel's religious life.

I
RELIGIOUS EXPERIENCE
AS INSIGHT

My examination of religious experience in the Old Testament will generally follow the analysis of religious experience developed in Part Two, focusing upon its impetus (conflict), character (perceptual shift), and direction. I will begin by looking at the role of conflict heightening, how this serves as an impetus to restructuring, and what specific devices may serve to evoke a perceptual shift. I will then concentrate on the thematization of the perceptual shift in symbolic language and conclude the section with a consideration of the manifestation of the perceptual shift in action.

A
Conflict Heightening and Restructuring

Experiential theology suggests that the primary task of both the lived experience behind the text and of the text itself is not to provide authoritative answers to questions concerning "reality" and our existential conflicts. Rather the purpose is to stimulate in the participant the type of perceptual shift discussed in Part Two which opens a person to new possibilities of action. To accomplish this, a situation of conflict is necessary. As suggested in the preceding chapter, this conflict may be contained within the narrative to the extent that the reader identifies with both parties to the conflict.[1] Or conflict may be sharpened between the audience and the speaker (author), most commonly by the prophetic oracle. It goes too far to say that the conflict is created. Conflict is endemic to the human situation. The prophet—whom we shall speak of paradigmatically as the characteristic assumer of this conflict-heightening role in Israel—rather brings into consciousness conflicts which are already latent in the audience, conflicts which the society tries to gloss over because they are irresolvable.

Let us consider some specific examples. Since the conflict is more reexposed than created by the prophet, the traditional key question of the relationship between prophecy and the principal traditions such as Zion and Exodus is also an important question for us. Often the question is asked as to whether the prophet is radical or conservative. If by conservative we mean conservative of the existing order and its world view by reifying it and making it part of the unchangeable givens, the prophets are certainly radical. Indeed, just this is a useful operative distinction between the false and the true prophets. The false prophets are the system-maintaining prophets, the "shalom" prophets, who try to blur the contradictions and conflicts within the system.[2] Against this the true prophet speaks the word of "no peace" (Jeremiah 6:14; 8:11; Ezekiel 13:10). But if by conservative we mean that the prophet depends on tradition, they are conservative. The perceptual shift involves not a replacing of one group of data with another but rather a basic restructuring of the same material. The prophets do not simply come into the situation with a message out of an ontologically transcendent other realm. The prophetic approach to tradition which I call inversion may be compared to the figure-ground reversal of Gestalt psychology. Most commonly a positive tradition is inverted into a negative one. The "Day of Yahweh"'s salvation becomes the day of judgment. The expectation of security in Zion is either denied (Jeremiah 7) or Zion itself is said to be the source of the stumbling of the people (Isaiah 8:14-15). Ezekiel 15-23 reads as an almost systematic effort to invert all the salvation traditions of the people, most dramatically in chapter 20 where the "salvation history" is changed into "unsalvation" history. The inversion need not be from positive to negative. Second Isaiah takes the prophetic lawsuit which had been used exclusively to announce judgment on Israel and utilizes it to proclaim the coming judgment on the nations leading to salvation for Israel. This inversion is not a simple mechanical reversal in which everything negative is turned into a positive and everything positive is turned into a negative, with the result that the basic structure remains the same. If this were so, creative prophecy would be quite a simple process for anyone—ancient Israelite or contemporary man—who was willing to pay the price or reap the reward resulting from society's response to the act of inverting the sacred traditions. Rather the inversion results in a genuine transformation of the tradition which keeps the traditional elements but alters their structural basis.

Another conflict-heightening device is the barring of irreconcilable conflict between different institutions. In the story of Naboth's vineyard (1 Kings 21), the conflict is revealed as between normal patterns of kingship with rights of "eminent domain" over the land and the amphictyonic tradition which assumes an inalienable tribal and clan inheritance. The conflict is thematized in the different words applied to the plot of land: the king who wants it and offers a very reasonable price refers to it simply as a "vineyard"; Naboth in his refusal refers to it as "the inheritance of my fathers."[3]

The conflict may also arise out of differing world views or from a lack of fit between the basic systems of the culture.[4] To limit ourselves to one example, in Ezekiel 18 the people complain that the children are suffering for the sins of their fathers. The people regard this as unjust. But also they believe that it is part of the world as it exists. This common perception of reality, especially rooted in wisdom circles, is related to the cultural system. This complaint is countered by Ezekiel, who heightens the conflict by opposing to it a legal maxim derived from the societal system: The individual shall suffer for his own sins.[5] The conflict is then shifted onto a different level as the prophet shows that the people suffer for their own sins. Then the claim that God is not just is inverted into the counter-assertion that it is "your ways that are not just" (see Ezekiel 18:25-30).

What faces the prophet is not simply the necessity of giving a new solution or of feeding in new data which will cause reasonable people to see that they are wrong. The more entrenched and ideological their world view, the more likely the people are to filter out those elements which do not fit their perceptual scheme.[6] This selective filtration may throw new light on the common theme that the prophet is sent to speak to a people who will not hear him. The theme of nonhearing occurs in the call of Isaiah, Jeremiah, and Ezekiel—all the prophets for whom we have an explicit call narrative—showing its continuity and centrality.[7] The people are by and large incapable of hearing the prophet. The prophetic heightening of conflict, instead of introducing new data, may rather draw into consciousness some elements which have been in the background, providing a matrix for a restructuring of the addressee's perceptual system.

Thus we are led to conclude that what is most significant in the prophets in particular and in the Old Testament in general is not simply new data, better answers, or an analysis which corresponds more fully to an external reality—even if all three of these may have been thought to be crucial by the participants in the events (and indeed may have been important). This observation corresponds to the shift from knowledge to experience characteristic of religious encounter in experiential theology. Thus I will try to buttress somewhat further the importance of a focus as much or more on the structure (the how) of what is being said and its functional goals as on the content and its validity or reality-congruence. Claude Lévi-Strauss's observation concerning myth that structure takes precedence over content is equally applicable to the restructuring process of the perceptual shift.[8] For poetry also, what matters most is the structure and not the content. We must avoid a form-content dichotomy. Structure unites form and content, overcoming the analytical dichotomy which has plagued critics since the time of Plato and Aristotle. Structure focuses the unity of form and content in the perceptual shift. What is being said *is* the way it is being said and this way leads toward insight. In his book *Formula, Character, and Context,* William Whallon has pointed out that perhaps not a phrase of Hebrew Old Testament poetry is self-created; rather the words, phrases, and clauses are all traditional and the prophet and poet puts them together differently.[9] Both the poem and the biblical oracle as well as the biblical story, if translated into discursive statements of cognitive content, often turn out to appear rather trivial.

The restructuring may change nothing at the content or surface level. An example occurs in the story of Elijah's raising the son of the Phoenician woman (1 Kings 17:17-24). A key phrase of the opening of the pericope, "O man of God (v. 18)," is taken up in the conclusion when the woman confesses that "Now I know that you are a man of God, and that the word of the Lord in your mouth is truth [or, is truly in your mouth]." One might ask: What type of climax is this when the woman states at the end only what she had already stated at the beginning? An equally good example is found in the account of Elijah's encounter with Yahweh in the theophany on Mount Horeb. In verses 9-10 the complaint of Elijah is set forth in response to a question of Yahweh. The theophany follows, and it in turn is followed by a repetition of the question and complaint. Although there is no change in knowledge, the experience of the theophany has brought about a restructuring which enables Elijah to act (verses 15ff.) whereas he was unable to do so previously.[10] Similarly Job's experiencing of the theophany of God does not solve his problems as to his suffering or answer his questions as to the nature of God. Rather the perceptual shift renders the possibility for growth and action despite the existence of the problems.

So far we have been discussing the heightening of conflict only in terms of the presumed situation of original historical encounter. Obviously to us as readers of the biblical text—and to most of Israel as hearers of it—even more important is how this conflict heightening operates in the narrative or other type of text which is a mediated account of a historical (Elijah on Mount Carmel) or fictional original encounter (Noah flood story, Genesis 6—8). Is there any particular structure of the narrative, any narrative type, which is particularly adapted to this conflict-generating function? For the Old Testament the necessary research has not been done. Discourse analysis is still generally in its infancy. However, Roland Barthes' comments are suggestive. His third type of discourse—narrative and historical—"attempts to reproduce the structure of dilemmas actually faced by the protagonists."[11] In this light it is important to note the presence in many conflict narratives of a *perception-challenging statement.* Such is the address of Jezebel to Ahab in the story of Naboth's vineyard: Now be King (1 Kings 21:7). Another example from the Elijah cycle is the challenge of Elijah to the people (not to the Baal prophets!) in the contest on Mount Carmel: "How long will you go limping with two different opinions? If the Lord is God, follow him; but if Baal, then follow him (1 Kings 18:21)." This challenge brings out conflict by proposing a new question: not *whether* Baal and (or) Yahweh are *gods,* but *which* of them is *God.* In the story of the raising of the son of the Phoenician woman a similar role is played by the statement addressed to Elijah: "What have you against me, O man of God? You have come to me to bring my sin to remembrance, and to cause the death of my son! (1 Kings 17:18)." Such statements not only challenge the perceptions of one of the characters in the narrative but also generate an analogous conflict in the audience to whom the story is directed.

Since this use of narrative seems highly developed, why is it that the prophetic traditions more and more come to focus on the oracle—most commonly on the two-part doom prophecy (invective-threat) introduced by "thus says the Lord"? If the purpose of the biblical text were only to preserve for historical record accounts of past conflict encounters, narrative would be sufficient, although we shall have to come in the next chapter to the historical genesis of the use of narrative. Before trying to suggest an answer to the question of why the shift in prophecy from narrative to oracle, I should first sketch this shift briefly. In the eighth century prophets, narrative, and oracle stand side by side, with the dominant part being oracle. By the early sixth century, the oracle in the frame of the "word event" ("and the word of God came to me") dominates the book of Ezekiel. Formally the book is a narrative, but in fact there is practically no independent narrative. Slightly later we find the situation reversed in Isaiah 40—55, where narrative elements are present only in the context of an oracle. One factor in this development from narrative to oracle may have to do with the openness of the oracle. The narrative may be structured in such a way as to generate conflict conducive to perceptual shift. But its very having a definitive conclusion makes it more a closed structure —and thus closer to an answer given on the basis of someone else's experience—than is the oracle. The oracle can both thematize the conflict and provide expressive resources for the restructuring process without at the same time overdetermining the outcome of the restructuring.[12]

Another means used to evoke restructuring—again it cannot compel it—is the *self-conviction* device. A situation is created in which the person is led along step by step in an analysis in which he wholeheartedly concurs, until at the final point he suddenly finds that unknowingly and unwillingly he has "convicted" himself. Nathan thus uses the story of the rich man and the poor man's lamb to bring David to pronounce judgment on himself in the death of Bathsheba's husband (2 Samuel 12). Joab similarly secures the recall of Absalom, David's son, from exile in 2 Samuel 14 by having the woman of Tekoa relate an incident of fratricide to David. What takes place is analogous to what has been suggested as the essence of good poetry, which leads the reader along in a building sequence of expectations so that immediately before the end of the line he can predict the final word or meaning with certainty, only to discover that the poet has used this very expectation to say something different and bring the reader to a type of insight which he would not otherwise have experienced.[13] In the opening of the book of Amos the people expect a series of invectives against the surrounding nations to culminate in a blessing on themselves. Instead the series concludes with an oracle of even more severe judgment (2:66ff.) against Israel. Although these are well-known examples, the device as a whole needs systematic study.

Let us look at two additional examples from the Elijah cycle. In 2 Kings 1, the king sends a messenger to the god Baal-zebub to inquire whether he will recover from his sickness. The messengers are intercepted by Elijah, who gives them an answer which is twice repeated in the pericope. The perceptual shift in the story comes from perceiving the oracle simply as an answer to a normal inquiry to perceiving it as an oracle of judgment. When perceived as a response to an inquiry, the king desired to seize Elijah in order to try to change the situation. But when Elijah appears in the king's presence and the oracle is repeated the last time, the king who has expended so much effort to get his hands on Elijah does nothing. Why? Because perceiving now that he had misconstrued the oracle and that it is in fact a judgment oracle, there is nothing left for him to do. Action here takes the form of a change of direction of an anticipated action; literally, the action is no action.

Another example of "self-conviction" leading to perceptual shift is found in the story of Naboth's vineyard (1 Kings 21). The story as told suggests not that King Ahab schemed to get rid of Naboth but rather that he was unaware of his wife's action. His appearance to take possession of the vineyard after Naboth's death was, in terms of his own consciousness, completely justified. The context of the king so determined his perception of events that only the confrontation with Elijah caused him to experience a complete restructuring of the events and perceive differently his involvement.[14] Then he can only respond to Elijah: "Have you found me [out], O my enemy?" (1 Kings 21:20).

In Ezekiel 18 we saw both how a conflict was heightened by contrasting elements from two different systems and also how Ezekiel subsequently shifted the conflict to a still different level. Here the shift occurred in the actual development of the pericope. But a similar conflict-generating shift of level may involve the two levels of the audience's preunderstanding of a concept or a traditional tale and the different level represented by the prophet's or narrator's own understanding without the account involving as part of its story line an explicit shift from one level to another. In this case the shift of level is evoked in the audience (perceptual shift) under the influence of the pericope rather than narrated within the pericope. On a broad cultural level, an example of the restructuring of a concept is the change in the understanding in Israel of holiness. What previously had been thought to be holy (anything connected with the gods and the world of the gods) is now perceived to be defiling. What is holy becomes only Yahweh and, by extension, what is connected with him, including his people. The restructuring of this basic concept involves an implicit challenge to the metaphysical and ontological presuppositions of the ancient Near Eastern world view.

The shift in level may also involve an entire narrative. A well-known narrative is restructured by the narrator. The story becomes a unit drawn from a higher-order lexicon which the author can use to deal with different conflicts. Again the author utilizes the tension between the reader's knowledge of the "normal" use and the author's different application. The shift of level is from the original level of the audience (normal use) to the different level of the speaker. The analogy of the surface-deep structure distinction of transformational linguistics may help clarify what is involved. At the surface level two different sentences may be intuited to say the same thing. We would say that both are derived from the same deep structure. An example is the active and passive statements: "John ate the cake," "The cake was eaten by John." But two sentences with identical surface structure may derive from two different deep structures. An example from Noam Chomsky is "Flying planes can be dangerous" which may mean either "It is dangerous to fly planes" or "Planes which are flying can be dangerous." Just as two identical surface sentences may relate to two different deep structures, so the same basic narrative can relate to two different deep concerns. For example: the Elijah cycle, utilizing the plot of the raising of the dead boy by Elisha (2 Kings 4), changes both characters and context (1 Kings 17:17-24). The Elisha version presupposes an answer to the basic question raised in the Elijah version: What is it to be a prophet in Israel?

The shift in levels involving both the restructuring of a narrative and of a concept can be illustrated by the Yahwist's retelling of the Noah flood story, a story well known to his audience in earlier versions. The Yahwist restructures the story, partly by changing the sequence so that the statement of Noah's righteousness no longer comes at the beginning. The restructuring involves a double shift of levels. (1) The meaning of righteousness is shifted from a cultic perspective brought by the audience from the pre-Yahwist tradition to an election perspective introduced by the Yahwist. (2) The deep conflict to which the surface story relates is shifted from the problem of the fate of a righteous individual in a deserved collective judgment to the problem of how the purpose of Yahweh was to be accomplished when there were no righteous individuals.[15] Note that this second shift does not solve the original problem but makes it considerably less debilitating.

I will close this section on conflict heightening and restructuring with a final general example. In the individual psalms of lament, toward the end of the psalm there is often a startling change of tone from lament to confidence (e.g., Psalm 22). Apparently this is due to an oracle spoken by prophet or priest at that point, although none of the psalms actually contains the oracle. Nothing objective happened to change the "situation," but the oracle acts as a catalyst which enables the person to put the pieces back together in a different way. That done, the practical consequences in terms of capacity for action are enormous.

B
The Thematization of the Perceptual Shift

The process of the change of perception is beyond our direct access. As discussed in Part Two, we can only look at the two different sides of it (before and after) and the conditions which facilitate the shift.[16] The insight gained may, however, be gathered into an *image or symbol*. Such an image expresses the synthetic dialectic discussed in chapter 3. The symbol may operate at several different levels of abstraction. What is the function of such an image? Georg Fohrer speaks of the prophetic experience of insight being preserved in the oracle which may develop in poetic language what is first only a visual image.[17] This suggests that one function of the image is to evoke a similar experience in the audience and to provide an interpretative matrix for the oracle or narrative. But it would be a fundamental error to conclude that the image is simply a heuristic device by which a clear nonlinguistic insight is made easier for another to share. Rather, the image is essential in order that the person who has experienced the perceptual shift be able to grasp his new insight. The image is the bridge by which the old and the new are connected, thus providing a means to reflect on and express the experience. Initially, without the metaphor there is no possibility of entertaining the insight.[18] As Claude Lévi-Strauss says, "Metaphor can change the world," that is, "our world," because it causes us to restructure fundamentally our perceptions.[19] Thus while the image or symbol does not equal the insight, neither is it a device which comes only after the insight is securely in hand.

One common manifestation of the synthetic dialectic is the ambiguous word or phrase. Due to its internal structure, such an ambiguous word can refer to both sides of the perceptual shift and thus thematize that shift.[20] For example, in Genesis 3:10 (KJV) Adam, after eating the fruit, responds to God's inquiry by saying, "I heard thy voice . . . I was afraid . . . I was naked . . . I hid myself." "I heard thy voice" refers both to the sound of Yahweh in the garden which Adam did hear and to the command of God which Adam did not "hear" (e.g., "obey" in Old Testament Hebrew). The ambiguity in each of the four statements reveals to the audience that Adam has yet to experience insight.[21] Another example occurs in the theophany experience by Elijah on Mount Horeb (1 Kings 19) where there is a shift of meaning between the voice of verse 12 (primarily atmospheric denotation) and the voice of verse 13 (the normal denotation of an utterance), with the verb "to hear" linking the two usages (verse 13a). A more general example of an ambiguous image is the "remnant" with its dual thrust of "a remnant will be *saved*" and "*only* a remnant will be saved." It depends upon the person's own structuring of the situation which of the two is dominant. A similar ambiguity is present in the Immanuel sign ("God with us") given in the encounter between Isaiah and the king of Judah in Isaiah 7.

Closely related to the symbolic power of ambiguity is that of *paradox* and *enigma*. René Wellek has pointed out that one of America's outstanding literary critics, Cleanth Brooks, finds the use of tensions expressed particularly through incongruity, paradox, and irony to be the key to understanding all complex (and hence good) poetry.[22] One Old Testament example occurs in the account of the conversation between Yahweh and Moses, prior to the people's departure from Mount Sinai (Exodus 33). In verse 13 Moses says, "If I *have* found favor . . . show me now thy ways . . . that I *may* . . . find favor." Despite its prose form, the dynamics of this passage are much closer to a poem than to a discursive presentation of a logical problem leading to a logical resolution.[23]

Earlier I said that the image or symbol stands in a dialectical relationship both to the insight experience which produces it and to the fuller literary unit which aims to provoke a similar insight experience in others. A particular manifestation of this relationship is what I call the *kernel oracle*. The term kernel oracle refers to what one might be tempted to call a summary statement of an oracle. An excellent example is Ezekiel 16:43: "Because you have not remembered the days of your youth, but have enraged me with all these things; therefore, behold, I will requite your deeds upon your head, says the Lord God." What is the relationship of such a short oracle—seemingly complete in itself—to its related (in this case, 16:1-42) fuller formulation whose content and form it so well recapitulates? Pending a fuller investigation, only some suggestions can be given here.

Ezekiel 16:43 is an example of a case where the kernel oracle is a fully separate entity. But a kernel oracle may be embedded within the fuller oracle. R.B.Y. Scott proposes that in Isaiah we find a number of "private oracles" which the prophet expanded for public proclamation.[24] Brevard Childs in his study of the Assyrian oracles in Isaiah focuses upon what he calls the "summary-appraisal" form which stands in a somewhat similar relationship to the full oracle as does Scott's "private oracle" but clearly is neither private nor chronologically anterior to the full oracle.[25] Klaus Koch in his analysis of the oracle of judgment on the individual finds as a constant element a final *"ki"* clause which characterizes the content.[26] In many other cases there appears to be a similar relationship of kernelization without the kernel oracle being formally set apart as in the foregoing examples (e.g., Ezekiel 5:11).

Moving beyond the kernelization of an individual oracle, there are longer kernel oracles which appear to kernelize a section of a book, as, for example, Ezekiel 28:25-26 in relationship to Ezekiel 25-29. Still more inclusively, various scholars have argued that certain oracles may be seen as summaries of an entire prophetic book. Georg Fohrer proposes this for Isaiah 1. Walther Zimmerli's treatment of Ezekiel 39:23-29 and Claus Westermann's discussion of Isaiah 40:1-11 suggest the same type of relationship.[27] The call narratives can be seen as kernelizations of the entire message of the prophet.

Clearly, as in the case of the self-conviction motif, the kernel oracle utilizes a variety of different forms and genres to serve the same or a similar function. If one were to consider it a genre in any sense—which is uncertain—it would have to be a middle-level rather than a primary-level genre. Also, rather than a genesis model which puts the kernel either as the source (e.g., the "divine word") of the full oracle (e.g., the "prophetic word") or the full oracle as the source of the summary, an analogy from transformational linguistics may provide a more helpful model as well as explain my use of the "kernel" terminology. A kernel sentence is one which, unlike the deep structure, can actually be produced at the surface level and is generated by a minimal number of obligatory transformational operations on the deep structure. It is the simplest type of sentence. Most surface sentences are not kernel sentences but rather are derived from the same deep structure as the related kernel sentence. The proposal is that structurally the kernel (or near-kernel) sentence stands in a similar relationship to a more complex surface sentence as the kernel oracle to its related oracle, chapter, book, or message. This suggests that in terms of distance the "insight" comes closest to a surface eruption in the kernel oracle or in kernelizing language in general. This structural explanation suggests that although the kernel oracle (when explicit) is logically prior to the fuller statement, the historical (chronological) relationship may vary from case to case.[28]

C
Insight Manifested in Action

The reader will recall that the consideration of religious experience in the Old Testament has generally followed the analysis of religious experience developed in chapter 2 where the perceptual shift was shown to be linked to a commitment/ action thrust in the direction of outwardness and openness. It remains for us to focus on this commitment/action dimension in Old Testament religious experience.

Robin Winks in *The Historian as Detective* warns concerning the two occupations of his title:

There obviously is a gap between politics and scholarship. Dean Rusk, once an academician, has reminded us of the latter gap by pointing out that while scholars argue toward conclusions, those in positions to determine policy must argue to decisions. Most detective fiction moves toward a conviction.[29]

Insight which the biblical material tries to evoke is also characterized not by conclusions but by decisions. This was so in the case of the encounter of Elijah with both Ahab after the Naboth incident and with Ahaziah where the action was "no action." In the contest of Elijah with the Baal prophets, the changed perception of the people ("Yahweh is God") leads immediately to killing all the Baal prophets (1 Kings 18:39-40, JB). The theophany to Gideon in Judges 6 leads to his tearing down the altar of Baal. That in both cases the "action" element may be added later to the narrative does not effect their evidencing an orientation toward action more than to knowledge. To this action orientation we may also relate the strong ethical thrust in prophets like Amos and Isaiah. The prophets, in denying the claims to ultimate ontological grounding of those "realities" (social, political, and ideological) which guide the actions of most men (as will be discussed in chapter 5), demand a change in action. To the extent that such ontological claims are false claims, the realism of an Ahab or Ahaz proves to be less realistic than the "idealism" of an Elijah or an Isaiah. As Peter Berger says in his discussion of the clown, Quixote's hope proves to be more realistic than Sancho's realism.[30] Thus (as Gerhard von Rad has shown for Genesis 15), faith in the Old Testament is not acknowledgment of dogma but action based on commitment to a new reality "as if" true.[31] Judaism has tended to dissolve this insight-action unity into an emphasis on action (including ritual action), while Christianity has often concentrated on reflection on the insight to the detriment of action.

To be sure, many actions of Old Testament men do not appear to be "outward" and "open." Further, the emphasis on action opens the way to two types of undesirable moralism—a concern with the "if-then" of the commandments or a concern with the elite status of particular groups or individuals. But these tendencies are recognized and combated in the Old Testament where the question is more "What must I do?" than "What must I do to be saved?" The rejection in the theophany on Mount Horeb of Elijah's excessive concern for himself ("I alone remain and they seek to kill me") displays both outwardness and openness (1 Kings 19:14ff.), as does the servant song of Isaiah 53.

Two pervasive Old Testament themes would seem to be particularly susceptible to such a moralism: election and covenant. The key to efforts to deal with this problem lies in the relationship of promise and imperative. Election can easily lead to an emphasis on status. In the Yahwist's interpretation of the election of Noah and Abraham, the relationship of promise and imperative is neither unconditional so that status is assured regardless of action (overemphasis of "insight") nor is it purely conditional in an "if-then" sense. Rather it is what Hans-Peter Müller calls "dialogic." Both Abraham (Genesis 12:1-3) and Noah receive a command (imperative) followed by a promise. This promise ("I will bless you") is in turn perceived as a further imperative ("be a blessing" to the peoples of the world). The dimensions of outwardness and openness are displayed, in that election is not exclusive and self-centered but for the entire world and its salvation.[32]

Covenant, on the other hand, is more open to the danger of the "if-then" distortion. If one keeps the commandments (action), then one will be blessed. But again this danger is recognized and combated. In the Priestly account of the covenant with Abraham, the only "commandment"—circumcision —is no commandment at all in the normal sense but rather the sign of the covenant by which a person confesses his adherence to this reality. More generally, Jean L'Hour has emphasized two factors which especially in the covenantal theology of Deuteronomy work against moralistic distortion.[33] The first is the relationship between the fundamental norm (which is highly general) and the specific commandments which are always incomplete actualizations of that norm. The second factor is the three-part structure of the covenant—past actions of God (promise), commandments (imperative), future blessings and punishments (promise). The blessing relates not only to the "if" of the commandment but is also directly related to the past acts of God in content and origin. The dynamic unity of these three elements makes any "if-then" understanding of the covenant a fundamental distortion. Thus while the Yahwist handles the problem of status moralism by putting the promise within the context of an imperative-promise-imperative sequence, Deuteronomy handles the dangers of "if-then" moralism by putting the imperative within the context of a promise-imperative-promise sequence. This means there is no easy out, no clear answers.

II
THE EXPERIENTIAL ORIENTATION
OF OLD TESTAMENT SPEECH

The discussion of the text and its role in evoking religious insight indicates that the use of language is a crucial question for experiential theology. This question has been considered in chapter 3 in terms of the semantic, analogic, and synthetic dialectics. In this section I will begin with some general observations about current study of language which have important implications for interpretations of the Bible from the perspective of experiential theology. Then I will look more specifically at some indicators of an a-metaphysical orientation in the Old Testament's use of language and at some counter-tendencies toward the reification of language.

A
The Study of Language: Implications for
Biblical Interpretation from the
Perspective of Experiential Theology

In their recent book addressed primarily to those whose task it is to translate the Bible into the different written and spoken languages of the world, Eugene Nida and Charles Taber remind us of the varied purposes served by language in communication:

It would be wrong to think, however, that the response of the receptors in the second language is merely in terms of comprehension of the information, for communication is not merely informative. It must also be expressive and imperative if it is to serve the principal purposes of communications such as those found in the Bible. That is to say, a translation of the Bible must not only provide information which people can understand but must present the message in such a way that people can feel its relevance (the expressive element in communication) and can then respond to it in action (the imperative function).[34]

Indeed, the information aspect of language may often be distinctly secondary. Susanne Langer distinguishes discursive (e.g., in a logical treatise) from presentative (e.g., in a poem) use of language. The first leads to knowledge, the second to insight. This (and similar distinctions by others) provides theoretical support for the approach of experiential theology to the Bible which would seek in the Bible not only or even primarily a truer knowledge (i.e., putting the emphasis on discursive use of language).

Language is an important subject matter of a number of different disciplines. Of these, the contributions of philosophy, literary criticism, and linguistics are of central importance for the biblical interpreter. Until recently these three disciplines went their own largely independent ways, culminating in the works of the linguistic philosophers on language (e.g., Ludwig Wittgenstein), of the New Critics on literature (e.g., I.A. Richards, William Empson, Cleanth Brooks), and of the descriptive linguists on nonliterary language (e.g., Leonard Bloomfield). In this stage of independence it was generally philosophy which pushed furthest in consideration of meaning, a topic intentionally avoided by descriptive linguistics. When the results and methods of these primary disciplines were appropriated for biblical interpretation, there was even less contact between them. Probably philosophical discussions of language exercised the greatest influence, especially in discussions of hermeneutics among the Bultmannians and the developers of the New Hermeneutic. Some New Hermeneuticians have more recently been influenced also by New Criticism, with its emphasis on the text as an independent entity. But as Donald Freeman has pointed out, literary criticism has recently begun to move away from concentration on the text as an isolated entity to the reconstruction of the author's explicit and implicit motives.[35]

Similarly, linguists have added to their traditional concern for an empirical description of the surface structure of the language a consideration of the generation of the sentence from the deep level of meaning and have also begun to expand the unit of analysis beyond the sentence. Linguists have also taken up the discussion of the philosophical implications and presuppositions of their work (e.g., Noam Chomsky). Thus while the three disciplines more and more interact and overlap, the appropriation of results into biblical study suffers a kind of generation gap.

What are the implications of this renewed interaction for the understanding of biblical texts? Obviously this is not the place to give a full answer. However, I would suggest that a crucial problem both theoretically and at the practical level of the interpretations of specific texts is how to relate to one another different perspectives on language, uses of language, functions of language, and expressions of language. These points of interaction I call juncture points.

Four types of juncture points will be noted. The first juncture is between the different types of "meaning" which a word can have and how these various types of meaning interact in a text.[36] The second juncture point concerns the relationship between the surface structure and the deep structure which generates it, a crucial topic for transformational linguistics. The area of semantics which linguistics so long ignored appears to be particularly linked with the deep level. The third juncture is between the different functions of language in a text, including most obviously the referential, emotive, connotative, metalingual, and poetic functions.[37]

While the preceding three types of juncture involve points of contact within an area, the fourth juncture is between different levels of analysis and expression of the text. The relation of the results of linguistic, stylistic, form-critical, and content (meaning) analysis becomes increasingly problematical as each expands beyond its traditional areas of concentration.[38] The significance for experiential theology of concentration on these juncture points is that it seems likely that it is at and by utilization of such junctures that the "potentially creative symbolic" character of language is actualized.

B
The Old Testament Use of Language

James Barr and others have emphasized that there is no necessary congruence between language and thought. Yet, as Nida and Taber point out, it would be folly to overlook the very real differences between languages.[39] Specific languages have distinctive characteristics of vocabulary, word formation, and syntax which influence both thought and expression. Many characteristics of Hebrew are shared with other Semitic languages. Amos Wilder notes as characteristics of Hebrew narrative the verbal orientation, the paratactic syntax, the minor role of adjective and description, the use of dialogue, and an emphasis on action.[40] While Akkadian, the basic language of Mesopotamia, is a related Semitic language, it is influenced by a non-Semitic substratum, Sumerian. The earlier Mesopotamian myths are written in Sumerian. Naturally the Egyptian myths are in a non-Semitic language. Thus the linguistic environment of Israel, while similar to its immediate neighbors, differs significantly from that of the three dominant cultural centers of Mesopotamia, Egypt, and Anatolia.

Hans Schmid distinguishes Hebrew (Canaanite) language from Israelite language.[41] It would be less confusing, however, to distinguish Hebrew (the "langue" of the descriptive linguist) from the characteristic *use* made of Hebrew by Israel (the "parole" or "speech" of the linguist), including what functions of language and aspects of meaning are emphasized. Geo Widengren has noted the speculative element involved in mythological use of language.[42] Old Testament use of language tends to be distinctly *nonspeculative* and focuses more on the connotative and poetic functions than on the informational and referential functions, *a first indication of its a-metaphysical orientation.* Even with such a seemingly referential category as names, James Barr says that in Old Testament narrative the connotation is almost always more significant in the literary usage of the name than the denotation.[43] This is most obvious in the turning back of metaphysical speculation about the ontic grounding of the experience expressed as an encounter with God. As was noted in chapter 2, the concern for the "nature" of God in Exodus 3:14 is rejected by the author. The verse utilizes a play on the name Yahweh ("I will be") to connote both the patriarchal traditions ("I will be with you" is a typical promise of the nonplace-bound god of the religion of the patriarchs) and the covenantal-Sinai traditions ("I will be your God" is one half of the "covenant formula"). This juxtaposition is a use of the poetic function to link the two traditions. Similarly, the accounts of the effort of Jacob to secure the name of the angel with whom he wrestles at Penuel (Genesis 32:29) and of Manoah to secure the name of the angel who appeared to him (Judges 13:17) stand out in their rejection of speculation into the "real meaning" of the divine name. This does not only protect God from manipulation. In all three cases the name is both revealing and concealing. It refers to an experience of man symbolized as an action of God but rejects emphasis on the referential implications of the name (e.g., where does he live? since when?) apart from the experience.

It is no coincidence that in both the Priestly and Elohist narratives the name Yahweh is revealed first at Exodus and Sinai, the most significant event in their reading of Israel's history. The Yahwist author, who downplays the exodus event, utilizes the name Yahweh from the beginning. Other cases in which a name serves to express the intensity and authority of the material are the ascription of all law to Moses, of all the proverbs to Solomon, and of all the psalms to David. In all these cases the referential function is not entirely absent and the more important emotive function presupposes the prior referential aspect: Solomon was historically linked with the wisdom movement, Moses with legal traditions, and David with cultic psalmody. Here the referential function is necessary historically but does not correspond to the basic intent behind the present usage.

A second indicator of an a-metaphysical tendency is that, in referring to events which do have a historical referent, the referential function is often not the most important in the author's use of language. In the reference to Jael who killed the Canaanite general Sisera, grabbing "a tent-peg with her hand, a mallet with her right hand," William F. Albright argues that the strictly literalistic referential reading of Judges 4:21 was a false literalization of the poetic language of the older tradition found in 5:26.[44] In the description of the event at the Reed Sea, the older tradition tells referentially neither how it happened, where it happened, or when it happened (at the "sea" Yahweh "shot" the Egyptians into the sea). This does not imply a lack of concern with history. The purpose is to testify to an event which once brought about a perceptual shift and to utilize the emotive, connotative, and poetic functions of the language so as to evoke a similar experience in the hearer rather than primarily to convey accurate cognitive knowledge about the event.

The third indicator is the secondary role of etiology, as recently demonstrated for the Pentateuch by Burke Long.[45] This is to be contrasted to the basic etiological form and paradigmatic intent of myth where the categories are the "real" things. A fourth manifestation of the a-metaphysical tendency is the relatively insignificant role of the predictive element in Old Testament prophecy. To predict in the ancient Near Eastern context presupposed a knowledge of what was happening in the "other world" as the macrocosmic determiner of what happens in this world. Omen and astrological literature by which the signs of coming events were perceived is strikingly absent from the Old Testament in contrast to their central role in Mesopotamian culture. Attention in Israel is focused on the doing of men, not on happenings in the world of the gods. The concept of the sign, while retained by the Old Testament, is understood out of the sphere of human relations in which one person gives a pledge to assure another person of his word or action. Often the sign occurs only in the future as one participates in the event to which the sign testifies. The sign given to Moses (Exodus 3:12) to encourage him to bring out the people is that he and the people will worship God on Sinai *after* the exodus. The Immanuel sign given to King Ahaz (Isaiah 7) is likewise a future sign which will occur only after the king and people have committed themselves to a specific course of action. Behind this important but seemingly paradoxical downplaying of the predictive element in Old Testament prophecy and Israelite religion lies a basic perceptual shift within Israelite culture as a whole which is the topic of the next chapter. These indicators of an a-metaphysical orientation in the Old Testament's use of language suggest a current within ancient Israel which fits well with the analysis of religious language from the perspective of experiential theology found elsewhere in this volume.

C
Reification of Language

To say that there was a tendency to react against metaphysical speculation and a relative deemphasis in religious language of the referential function does not deny the existence of counter-tendencies toward the reification of language. Five such tendencies can be noted, although we should remember that in any specific case only the consideration of the entire communicative situation makes it possible to determine whether the language has been reified. The first tendency is toward the hypostatization of originally metaphoric and poetic language. Obviously the borderline is nebulous and hypostatization is more than simple personification. An example is the development of the figure of Satan from a function ("the accuser") to a specific transcendent being. As Max Black points out, this "hypostatization of entities" is facilitated in languages like Greek and English which, unlike Hebrew, freely form nominalizations (e.g., re-forming an underlying verbal clause as a noun phrase) and hence can easily formulate the question of meaning as "to what thing does X refer?"

The second tendency is related to the first and involves an objectification in which it is assumed that all words refer to a real entity which can be located in place, time, and attributes.[46] For example, the covenant language expressing the relationship between Yahweh and Israel is objectified in terms of the treaty pattern which leaves no place for a continued relationship once the treaty is broken. Hence there arises in the exile (a result of the "treaty" being broken) a crisis which leads the Priestly author to abandon treaty-type covenantal language (Genesis 9:17), while Jeremiah and Ezekiel speak of a "new covenant" grounded differently. This is itself a case of creative insight coming from the conflict caused by the encounter of historical events with an overly objectified understanding of older religious language. Amos Wilder speaks of "a continuing revolution against unreal categories" being found in the Bible.[47]

The third tendency is to literalize language. The originally secondary aspects of reality-congruence and designation are pressed by the later tradition, which more and more "literalizes" and expands the implications of this literalization as already mentioned in Judges 4:21. Such literalization occurs in writings which emphasize the fulfillment of prophecy. The "sun stands still" oracle spoken by Joshua at the battle of Gibeon during the period of the Judges (Joshua 10:12) provides a striking example. Originally, the reference was to a "convergence" of sun and moon, which would prognosticate the outcome of the battle. A later commentator took the language literally and supplemented the story accordingly.[48] Wilder mentions a similar process of literalization of the appearance of Jesus to the disciples in the boat on the Sea of Galilee.[49]

Fourth, in a related process, accounts of events whose language was primarily nonreferential are supplemented subsequently with the details of what "actually happened." Thus the later accounts of the events at the Reed Sea try to tie down the event in terms of what happened and where it happened. Roland Barthes discusses this "reality effect" present in a type of historical writing which claims to reconstruct the events by using language purely referentially.[50]

The fifth tendency toward reification of language makes the metalingual function (language about language) paramount. Language, cut off from the depth roots which originally called it forth, becomes dogmatized as an approach to experience which prevents rather than leads to insight. This is exemplified in the arguments of the friends of Job concerning Job's misfortunes when they take previous insights into human experience preserved in the wisdom tradition and use them as ossified categories which are imposed on Job's experience and distort it. This tendency within wisdom tradition has been discussed by Hans Schmid. Wilder discusses a similar development in the late pre-Christian period as it applies to the increasingly juridical treatment of the law.[51] Rejection of speculation concerning the name Yahweh may be regarded as a refusal to enter into a metalingual discussion of its meaning. To the extent that they become language about the language of the text and are divorced from the experiential basis of the text, both Christian theology (and exegesis) and the great Jewish commentaries (such as the Talmud and Bereshith Rabbah) exemplify the potential danger of concentration on the metalingual function.

At the opposite pole, the tendency is to mystify the language by emptying it of all specific content. This trivialization of language leads to the sloganitis noted in chapter 1. An example is Judges 6:7-10, a collage of clichés taken from various sources. Trivialization can be simply a playing with words, just as may be a discussion of meaning at a metalingual or theological level. Yet the very emptying of words of their cognitive content may enable them to link up once again with the primordial (prereflective) levels of experience and thus evoke a perceptual shift in the audience. This is characteristic of the Deuteronomist historian (Deuteronomy through Kings). Sibley Towner points out that it is also characteristic of the language of Martin Luther King ("I have a dream"), where, however, the emotive and connotative functions combine with a strongly developed poetic function resulting in a symbolic and (to use Langer's terminology) "presentational" use of language.[52] Here language functions analogously to music which may lead to insight. But the experiential theologian would be obliged to point out that, as with music, so language which has been totally voided of content may also be correspondingly weak in its ability to evoke a genuine restructuring leading to action characterized by outwardness and openness. For the exegete the key task is to recognize in the specific text where the functional emphasis in the use of language falls. Often it will not be primarily at the cognitive, informational level.

In this chapter we have looked at some aspects of religious experience recorded in the Old Testament and at the use of language to express or evoke such experience. At times we have had occasion to make a contrast with myth, a consideration which will be developed more fully in the next chapter. The use of language in myth is also crucial. Myth has been called a way of expressing "a social dialectic. It stresses the salient social contradictions, restates them in more and more modified fashion, until in the final statement the contradictions are resolved, or so modified and masked as to be minimized."[53] While myth serves to gloss over and by logical dialectics remove the tension created by existential conflict, the Old Testament works through heightening of conflict to evoke a perceptual shift which frees one for new action. Myth is inauthentic because it is conservative of the existing world view and radically reductionistic. The thrust of Old Testament religious experience is to challenge existing perceptual structures and enable one to live with complexity.[54]

debunking and the open society: the reconstruction of reality in ancient israel

W. MALCOLM CLARK

In the preceding chapter the format of our approach to religious experience in Israel was largely suggested by the analysis of religious experience presented elsewhere in this volume. This meant a focus on the individual and case level, with particular attention to how language functioned to provide a suitable context for the perceptual shift which it was earlier asserted was characteristic of creative religious experience. In this chapter I will try to move to the "why" behind the "what" which we found in the last chapter. This involves a move from the personal and individual to the cultural and societal levels. My approach will largely take the form of a sweeping historical overview and analysis rather than explicit application of a model provided by experiential theology. Already the end of the last chapter began to move in this direction in discussing the Old Testament's a-metaphysical use of language and the a-mythical orientation of the Old Testament. Both of these topics are also central concerns of experiential theology, the latter because the model of experiential theology involves heightening of conflict while myth is oriented toward harmonizing and blurring conflict and contradiction. This line of investigation will be developed in this chapter as I take up the openness to experience crucial to experiential theology. I will attempt to link this to a similar openness in the Old Testament, an openness to be connected

124

with the movement from myth to history in Israel. This openness takes especially the form in Israel of a debunking orientation which denies the ontological claims of all humanly produced institutions and ideologies.

My approach is consistent with the presuppositions of experiential theology. This means that without trying to adjudicate the validity of Israel's own theological assertions, the point of departure must be Israel's own religious (and secular) experience. In particular I will look at the following: (1) the mythical world view as involving a massive reification of human ideologies and institutions; (2) the debunking thrust in Israel which denies the ontological claims of such ideologies and institutions; (3) the necessary historical and sociological conditions for dereification and the application of this to the early history of Israel; (4) the resulting openness to history as a source of insight and the "how" through which such openness found expression; (5) eschatology as a structural transformation of myth— myth's functional counterpart called forth by the (partial) demise of myth in Israel; and, finally, (6) a basic problem resulting from Israel's dereification of institutions and ideologies, the problem of norm and authority. This is equally a problem which experiential theology has to face if it claims to avoid an extreme relativism. Perhaps some of the suggestions as to how this problem of authority was faced in Israel without resorting to extreme relativism may offer insight into how to follow up some aspects of this question as it pertains to experiential theology in general, although it is not intended to develop such a feedback explicitly in this chapter.

I
THE OPEN SOCIETY:
ITS SOCIOCULTURAL CONTEXT

A
The Debunking Tendency in Ancient Israel
Peter Berger and Thomas Luckmann in *The Social Construction of Reality* utilize a sociology of knowledge perspective to analyze the strange phenomenon that, although social, cultural, and political forms are humanly produced, they are perceived by the individual as standing over against him as part of an

independent reality. Thus perceived, they are strongly resistant to change by man.[1] Elsewhere, Berger and Stanley Pullberg provide a useful characterization of this process of reification. They distinguish four processes: (1) Objectivation is the process whereby human subjectivity embodies itself in products available to oneself and one's fellowman. (2) Objectification is the moment in the process of objectivation when man establishes distance from his products and makes of them an object of his consciousness. Both of these two steps are natural to man as a world-producing creature. (3) Alienation is the process by which the product takes on a life of its own and is no longer recognized as a human product. Functionally, alienation provides protection against anomie. (4) Reification is the moment in the process of alienation in which the characteristic of thinghood becomes the standard of objective reality. Reality becomes the now objectified and abstracted production of human social productivity. Thus reification is a matter of consciousness, and here Berger and Pullberg distinguish three stages: (a) direct and prereflective; (b) reflective, in which the action or thing is seen as characterizing the person rather than as an expression of the person; and (c) theoretical, in which the results of the process of alienation and reification are given a theoretical justification (ideology).[2]

The mythical world view, such as we find it in the ancient Near East, is an archaic form of massive reification of the existent order by which that order is ontologically grounded in a reality outside of this world. As James Barr and others emphasize, this world stands in a correspondence relationship to the divine world (microcosm: macrocosm).[3] Etiology (explaining how things are by relating how they came to be in the primeval period) provides the form of much myth, but myth's function is to use this form as a logical tool to deal with existential contradictions man faces within his society. Myth not only mediates between this world and the divine world, it also mediates between man and his world. Thus it operates on both a vertical and horizontal axis, where the vertical axis is the language used to speak about the horizontal axis.[4] Myth is both inauthentic (due to its reification aspect) and abstract (due to its function as logic).

The basic thesis of this section is that a persistent element in Israel's religious life was a debunking factor which denied the ultimacy of any humanly constructed world order (whether or not conceived of as divinely instituted). The correlate of this debunking factor is a radical openness to experience.[5] We may call this orientation the basic perceptual shift in Israel as compared with the surrounding cultures. Because such an orientation is prereflective and pretheological, any significant uniqueness of Israel is not to be sought primarily at the level of specific conceptual beliefs.

Debunking first operates on the dominant mythological world view in an external thrust. The basic correspondences are radically altered. (1) God stands over against the whole cosmos rather than within one part of a binary cosmos. The assertion of the absolute otherness of Yahweh further eliminates the mediating categories: the semigods and minor divinities as well as the divine or near-divine king. (2) The redefinition of holiness breaks down the correspondence/separation of the mythical world view in terms of space. (3) The concept of holy time also undergoes a radical shift in which the sabbath, a nonfestival day, emerges as the crucial "religious" day in Israel. Thus Israel does not create any new myths and makes only limited use of existing ones.

Debunking also operates internally upon Israel itself. Secularization results from the refusal to grant ontological status to humanly constructed *institutions.* No single political order is seen as indispensable, just as none is seen as incompatible. An early example is the rejection of the claims of the Eli priesthood as represented in the Samuel traditions.[6] More far-reaching is the perspective on kingship as a human institution, subject to modification and abandonment. Also, the relativization of the significance of the sacrificial cult (not its rejection) in the prophets and the psalms reflects the same debunking tendency.

At the *cultural* level, debunking is exemplified in the prophetic attitude toward the major ideological traditions. The symbolic language of these traditions originated generally as a mode of expression of the insight experienced in the perceptual shift of a creative religious experience. Too often such symbolic language subsequently came to function as a legitimation of an established order. Thus functioning as an a priori and largely external means of interpreting new experience, the tradition and its symbols stood in the way of direct apprehension of new experience and closed off new insight which might result from openness to the experience. We are dealing here with the three levels of experience, language expressing the experience and ideological and theological reflection on the language expressing the experience (which may be either functional or disfunctional) which is discussed elsewhere in this volume. *When the language of the tradition has thus ceased to function primarily at the religious level of direct relationship to experience and has shifted to a primary link to the theological and ideological level (and the related metalingual function), then the prophetic debunking orientation is turned against it.* Such prophetic inversion of the traditions we have already discussed in a different context. The result may be rejection of the tradition involved. For example, George Coates has shown how the Yahwist source has used the motif of Israel's murmuring in the wilderness after the exodus from Egypt to demonstrate that Israel's former "election" in the event of the exodus is no longer valid. She must therefore depend on a new election event, the election of the Davidic monarchy.[7] Instead of outright rejection, the result may be reinterpretation. Thus, to continue the previous example, the Yahwist does not simply accept the traditional election ideology which was linked with and justified the special (exclusive) status of the king. Rather he freed election from its dependence on kingship, reinterpreted election inclusively in terms of service, and then on this basis reinterpreted the election of the king.[8]

Indeed, even mythic images once separated from their ideological (i.e., mythological) context and ontological implications can be reappropriated by the prophets. The mythic image is older historically and individually than is myth as connected narrative or system. Freed from the correspondence scheme, the mythic images may be used simply metaphorically or may reconnect as symbols with the primordial levels of human experience which originally gave birth to them without being reified. Thus Walther Zimmerli suggests that the account in Ezekiel 28 of the king of Tyre which is superficially much more mythological in language than the related account of Adam in the Garden of Eden (Genesis 2—3) is actually much less mythological because it no longer has any mythological function.[9]

What takes place in ancient Israel is not a single change (although there is certainly a cumulative effect) from an ideological system (myth) to a debunking system which becomes another ideology. Rather, there is a constant debunking process operative throughout Israel's history upon the continually strong human tendency to reify the socially constructed world. Because it is not a change from one ideology to another—from one content to another—but rather a change of perceptual structures, all efforts to find any one "center" for Old Testament theology (e.g., covenant, election, kingdom of God) are doomed, even if the center is a dynamic one such as "the way." Israel was to institutionalize the debunking critique without the critiquers taking over and turning their views into another ideology. The largely unique nature of prophecy in ancient Israel may rest upon its debunking function.[10]

B
The Historical Conditions

Why did this pervasive perceptual shift producing a debunking orientation (dereification) take place? Experiential theology suggests that we start with Israel's own experience rather than with an interpretative theological statement such as might say that it was God's decisive act for Israel in the exodus which led Israel to make a break with mythological modes of understanding and focus on history. Berger and Pullberg set forth three conditions for dereification: (1) anomie and the breakdown in which the system is revealed as only human by its failure to function smoothly; (2) cultural contact and shock, which provide alternative ways of perceiving reality; (3) dereifying tendency of individuals and groups existing in a situation of social marginality.[11] All three of these conditions are realized at the time of Israel's settlement in Palestine at the end of the Late Bronze age (late second millenium), a period decisive for Israel's subsequent self-understanding.[12]

First, it was a time of the breakdown of established systems all over the ancient Near East (or, in Egypt, their exhaustion) both culturally and politically. This breakup meant that the old myths were not any longer (and not yet again) able to speak directly to Israel.

Second, the condition of cultural shock was actualized by Israel's geographical location in Palestine where the Mesopotamian cultural heritage and the Egyptian political control were superimposed. Only during the second half of the second millenium did Egypt exercise effective political control in Palestine. Even if the difference of world views was not crystallized and explicit, yet the fact that individuals were living under a cultural system derived from one system and at least elements of a political system derived from another system made for a considerable lack of harmony and cultural shock. Israel recognized this situation in indicating both its Mesopotamian origins and its Egyptian bondage as decisive formative elements in its prehistory.

Third, Israel came from a situation of social marginality as defined from the perspective of the culture of the settled land into which it was to integrate itself and find its self-identity. Of course, this was true of each of the various waves of semi-nomadic clans penetrating from the fringes into the settled lands, as again illustrated at Mari. Normally these groups would simply be absorbed, both politically and culturally, by the dominant social reality and its reifying ideology. But the breakdown both of world order (and with it of the ideology which determined the perception of reality) as well as the presence of pseudo-alternatives meant that Israel neither was nor could simply be absorbed.[13] Social marginality was also significant for the continued debunking thrust in Israel. Both Elijah and Elisha came from the marginal area of Transjordan and Amos from a marginal area of Judah.[14]

C
From Myth to History

Since the mythological world view with its symbols was inoperative or insufficient, *how* was Israel to express her encounter with and perception of experience? The means "chosen" was history and narrative.[15] Primitive and archaic society with its massive reification expressed through myth does not recognize any change, certainly not as a positive value. It is no response to reply that in fact change took place in primitive society. Of course it did. The point is that the mythical world view by its claim to totality must constantly react to actual change by to some extent changing itself while all the while maintaining a facade that no significant change occurs. Only things which "fit" the ideology are perceived as significant and hence "real" happenings.[16] Sometimes one makes the distinction of dynamic and static societies, but Claude Lévi-Strauss's interpretation of society using the analogy of a machine may be more accurate. The mechanical machine (cold), which with a certain input of energy tends to run perpetually and remain in a state of equilibrium, corresponds to the primitive society. Opposed to this are the thermodynamic machines (hot) and societies which "work on the basis of a difference in temperature between their component parts."[17]

The problem is complicated by the varied meanings of the word history. Marc Gaboriau distinguishes (1) the history which man creates, (2) the history of men written by historians, which involves an individual interpretative stance (e.g., any modern "History of England"), and (3) the philosophy of history (e.g., Toynbee).[18] Primitive societies do have a history in the first sense, and this has to be dealt with in their equivalent to history in the third sense, a philosophy—so we might call it—of "no history." But this philosophy means that, while they may narrate happenings, they almost never write history in the second sense nor do they seek meaning in the course of history in the first sense. Mesopotamia had a view of history, that is, of time, which was part of its general world view, and so did Egypt: an implicit periodization as well as an orthodox sequence. But they failed to produce the historian's history. Different "theologies" were developed in the major cult centers, but it would be wrong to equate these with the genuine (if tendentious and selective) histories of the Yahwist, Deuteronomist, Elohist, Priestly, and other writers in Israel. Here is something approaching the second meaning of history: an interpretation of past events which gives significance to the elements of change and development in those events.[19] In Mesopotamia and Egypt annals were produced, as were chronicles and the other types of protohistoric writings such as royal letters to the gods, royal building inscriptions, and "naru" literature. All these related historical events but no interpretation of history. Mesopotamia had epic, but this is not the same as narrative.[20] Egypt approached somewhat closer to narrative as well as small-scale history in the Sinuhe "novel" and in the biographical tomb inscriptions. Yet in neither case was the purpose to seek meaning in history as such. Nor was it in the Hittite empire of Anatolia, which perhaps in texts such as the "apologies" came the closest to historical writing outside of the Old Testament.

Thus, although for particular purposes the archaic mind was well aware of the fact that things happen and that it was possible—and indeed, for various practical purposes, absolutely essential—to keep a record of some of these happenings, it is still possible to maintain that primitive thought is essentially "intemporelle" (timeless).[21] Even a historical event can function as a primeval event. There is no sharp distinction between "myth" as a literary genre concerning "unreal" events and literary genres which concern "real" events. The record of past events may contain a good deal of mythical influence just as, for example, as pointed out by J. Gwyn Griffiths, the Honus and Seth myth may reflect a good deal about the history of early Egypt. Bertil Albrektson is certainly correct when he says that it is not unique for Israel that God acts in history.[22] Rather, what is important is the manner of perception of the history in which God is perceived to be acting. The decisive stage comes not with the substitution of a historical event for a mythical event but rather when historical events are combined and it is the combination rather than the isolated units in which God is perceived to be acting. Only then does one cease to look for the reenactment of a past pattern or model and begin to be open for genuine new perception from historical experience. In Israel this happens when exodus, originally celebrated cultically by itself, is linked first with conquest and subsequently with the patriarchs.

The key change in Israel is that historical experience, whether personal or collective, is perceived as a message in a way that it was not in the rest of the ancient Near East. It is Israel's focusing on the message quality of the world seen diachronically (historically) which is significant for experiential theology and the debunking trend of Old Testament religion.[23] The turn from myth to narrative and history is a turn to experience as a source of insight. The question is: What is emphasized, the old or the new in experience? Eberhard Otto makes clear that in Egyptian narrative and "historical" writing, experience does not give rise to new insight (or at least is not believed to do so). Rather, everything is perceived in terms of traditional categories. Man reenacts certain roles, and what is emphasized in writings about events is how well he has fulfilled those roles.[24] David Maybury-Lewis notes that explanations by classification and explanations by history are mutually exclusive.[25] It is the classification approach to history which is characteristic of antiquity (e.g., the Sinuhe "novel") and of the mythological orientation. In Israel, there is at least a partial movement to explanation through history. Israel's historical structuring of experience is most clearly exemplified in the credos, those brief statements in which Israel capsulized its history (e.g., Deuteronomy 26:5-9). And these statements remain fundamentally open, able to be altered and expanded in the light of subsequent events. The orientation is to the new, so that even a theophany becomes not a reenactment of the old but an expression of new insight—literally a revelation. A similar distinction is seen when Israelite narrative and historical writing is compared with classical writings. As Erich Auerbach notes, the "realism" of biblical writings derives from their total openness to experience.[26] A result of this noncategorizing approach is the tendency to concentrate on "man." Thus God speaks to Adam ("man") and to Noah simply as to a man and not to them in the role of keeper of the holy garden and priest of the sanctuary respectively (which they were in pre-Israelite antecedents to these stories). Micah 6 concludes by saying, "He has showed you, O man, what is good (v.8)," while Ezekiel is addressed not as "prophet" but as "son of man" (i.e., "man"). The animals and plants in Genesis 1 are created according to their "kinds," but man is created simply as man. And even the king is first a man and only then a king so that Nathan can say to David, in convicting him of the murder of Bathsheba's husband Uriah, "You are the man (2 Sam. 12:7)."

The two approaches to historical experience would seem to

be mutually exclusive as ideal types. But we must also look for elements of continuity and ask what tools were available to our mythical first historian. The emphasis on experience brings to mind the wisdom traditions. There is in the Old Testament a large body of explicit wisdom literature (e.g., Proverbs, Job, Ecclesiastes), as well as varying amounts of wisdom influence in legal, prophetic, historical, and psalmic materials. This wisdom literature shows the greatest degree of commonality with the rest of the ancient Near East of any Old Testament material. One might argue that it is in the area of wisdom that the greatest openness to experience was found in the ancient Near East. Further, various studies have found significant wisdom influence in the Yahwist's history, in the Joseph novel, in the narrative of the succession to the throne of David, and in the later Deuteronomistic history. In short, my thesis is that it was in the intrinsically a-historical but experience-oriented wisdom traditions that the conceptual tools were found which were applied to the structuring of history in ancient Israel. Wisdom was the mediator or element of continuity in the turn from myth and categorization to narrative and history.

Let us consider the most characteristic wisdom genre, the wisdom saying (a middle-level type composed of various specific genres). The use of binary contrasts (e.g., fool and wise man) in Old Testament wisdom sayings may work as a conflict-heightening device so crucial in setting the stage for the possibility of the perceptual shift. The frequent conflict of the assertion of the saying with common sense (especially in Israel, where some of the more pragmatic concerns such as table manners received less emphasis) may further heighten the conflict. Such sayings may—as with Job's friends—represent an ossified approach to experience which reifies past insights and turns them into dogma. But they may also function as faith assertions which facilitate a changed course of action freed from the oppression of the massive reality presented by socially constructed institutions and ideologies.

Thus no genre is automatically open to experience or closed to it, although some may be more appropriate than others. The wisdom saying, together with the "novel," history, and oracle, form a genre field, one of whose defining characteristics is its orientation around experience. To avoid a too-simple equation of certain genres with Israel (e.g., history) and other genres with the rest of the ancient Near East, *we must make a functional and structural analysis of the entire genre field and make this analysis the object of comparison.* One result of the analysis of this genre field in Israel is the formula: saying:oracle::novel:history. On the one hand, saying and oracle share the quality of both being authoritative "words" while novel and history are both narratives. On the other hand, saying and novel are both personal and general while oracle and history are public and specific (unique). Further, the matrix suggests looking at the relationship between oracle and novel (prescriptive and descriptive) as well as that between saying and history (normative and interpretative).

A similar genre field occurs in Egyptian literature where novel, wisdom saying, history (apology), and prophecy intermix, with all showing a general influence from wisdom circles. A comparison of the fields shows, however, that in Egypt the approach is via categorization while in Israel it is via history. This attitude toward the "new" in experience is well illustrated by a comparison of Old Testament prophecies about disorder and chaos with those elements of Egyptian literature which have most often been compared to Old Testament prophecy: the "prophecies" about the disorders which occurred in the Intermediate Periods in Egypt when social and political order dissolved into anarchy. The Egyptian "prophet" can only look with horror on this period when a complete reversal took place in human affairs, when "the poor man rides a donkey while the formerly rich man walks." The Old Testament prophet looks forward with anticipation to the time when such a reversal will take place, when the high will be made low and the low high.

This brief analysis and comparison of two similar fields in Egyptian and Israelite literature warns us against making our cross-cultural comparisons only at the surface level when the functions and the deep structures may prove to be radically different. The shortcoming of the "myth and ritual" approach to the study of the Old Testament (e.g., Ivan Engnell, S.H. Hooke, and much "phenomenology of religion") is not its synchronic (a-historical) approach but rather that it compares only the surface structures (often in an atomistic fashion) and ignores the possibilities of different functional relationships between the similar parts, which difference would reflect different deep structures. Analogously, "demythologization" would often seem to strip away various cultural accompaniments to leave a core of content, but a core which is still at the surface level. Remythologization, a second step, implies also a surface-level procedure in which appropriate accompaniments are added to the core from the receptor language or culture. As discussed, for example, by Eugene Nida (and by Adda Bozeman using the example of the transmission of Buddhism to China from India), successful cultural translation must take account of deep-level meaning and structure and not be executed simply in a one-to-one correspondence fashion at the surface levels.[27]

One might ask to what extent the Hebrew language was adapted in the service of Israel's new orientation to experience. The presence of Hebrew as a relatively "new" language (a mixed language) may itself have provided an additional element of instability while enabling a certain freedom in its use. The distinctive feature of the Hebrew verbal system—the waw consecutive which served primarily a narrative function—correlates significantly with the turn to narrative and historical discourse as the primary mode of structuring reality. Once the basic change from a cold to a hot society is made, the change tends to be permanent despite all counterforces. This is so in part because the consciousness of history itself has a power of relativizing which hinders easy reification.[28] The effort to structure history creates a tension with views which arise out of man's typically older, synchronic efforts at structuring the world. Thus we have texts which speak both of the ontological status of Zion as chosen by God from the beginning while other texts speak of the election of Zion taking place only late in history and in a well-defined sequence of events. Israel's situation in which part of its political model was adapted by the monarchy from Egypt while the cultural basis remained firmly rooted in the Mesopotamian sphere created further continued disharmony within the system. In a longer study it would be necessary to deal more fully with Israel's transitional situation and with the counter-tendencies to those discussed above.

What we face in Israel is a process of change of perspective and of belief and not the clash of two fully formed, competing ideologies.

It would be strange to talk about the movement from myth to history without mentioning eschatology and apocalypticism—especially as it is generally agreed that a genuine eschatology is not found in any of the other ancient Near Eastern cultures. Two recent monographs have dealt with eschatology. Both accept Von Rad's position that eschatology involves the expectation of a new salvation event which, while analogous to the old, surpasses, negates, and fulfills it. Horst Preuss rejects various previous historical explanations, saying that the same conditions are found also among other ancient Near Eastern peoples. For Preuss, eschatology is the essence of Israel's experience with its God already from its patriarchal beginnings and implies a goal (teleological).[29] In contrast, Hans-Peter Müller finds that eschatology arises only within Israel's history. His thesis is that out of the experience of the aporia of the finality of the past intervention of God arose the expectation of a future, finally valid, intervention.[30] This was eschatology.

What does the perspective of experiential theology have to say to these two treatments? Müller's emphasis on the *experience* of the intervention of God is in the direction which experiential theology would wish to go. But ultimately, because it is a unique *transcendental* intervention which is seen to create the crisis which leads to eschatology, he can ignore the question of why it appears in Israel and not elsewhere.[31] Preuss, in trying to root eschatology in the historical beginnings of Israel's religion, at least addresses this question. But both his negative critique and his positive explanation are inadequate. He also ultimately eschews historically verifiable explanations and depends on Israel's experience of a unique intervention from a transcendental realm.[32]

Experiential theology, instead of concentrating on the transcendent's intervention, rather says that all we can examine is the experience which is expressed in this language. It also suggests that we look at the broader context which shapes that experience. We recall that a central task of myth is to mediate and resolve the contradictions which man encounters in his life and society. The question therefore arises: What functionally assumes in Israel this key task of myth (whose centrality means it must be handled in some way)? The proposed answer is: eschatology. Only instead of resolving the contradictions by logical dialectics (myth) which seem to make them disappear, eschatology heightens the contradictions by projecting them onto a "present-future" historical axis. Eschatology's positive value is both its heightening of the conflict and its potential to focus on the now of life as experienced rather than on either a macrocosmic other world or an escapism into the future. This suggests that Old Testament eschatology is not intrinsically teleological or goal-oriented. Thus my basic thesis is that with the rejection of a mythological world view, Israel turned to history (experience) as a means of self-understanding and to eschatology as a transformation of the handling of the contradictions of existence onto the historical dimension.[33]

The final question is: Why does apocalyptic literature appear when and where it does and not at the time of earlier crises such as the fall of the northern kingdom in 721 B.C.? What is changed when apocalypticism does appear is the creation of a basically new cultural shock and conflict situation. This time the resulting anomie·is too great to be assimilated within existent forms and symbols even to the extent that this had happened before. Previously it was a matter of developments within one basically similar ancient Near Eastern world view which was temporarily weakened and hence failed to absorb fully the emerging people Israel, although subsequently the system reintegrated itself and contained the disturbance. The encounter with Hellenism, in contrast, presented a challenge from without. Within Judaism there was a double conflict: first the continuation of the juxtaposition of the mythological and the developing historical perception; second, the new encounter with Hellenism. Thus in the overview we have the failure of myth leading to an openness to experience finding its literary expression in history and eschatology. Subsequently, a more massive challenge to the mythological system presented a double challenge to Israelite faith. Apocalypticism was the reaction at the literary level to the metaphysical orientation of Greek thought, while at the same time incorporating within itself elements of both history and eschatology as well as myth. Thus we may regard apocalyptic as a transformation of history and eschatology, a sort of narrated eschatology with a literalized and ontologized use of the old mythic language.

II
AUTHORITY AND NORM
IN THE OLD TESTAMENT

The question of authority has many dimensions, including the original authority of the speaker, the authority of what he says, the authority of the traditions and writings within the time span of the Old Testament, their authority for Jesus and for his contemporaries, and their authority for us.[34] More generally the question of authority and norm is a crucial one in the modern world, where all authorities and norms are brought into question. As has been mentioned, it is also a problem to be faced by experiential theology. Our immediate concern in this section, however, is the problem of authority and norm within ancient Israel. The sources of the problem should by now be clear. The dereification of the cultural and social world meant that the norms and authority could not be based in a microcosmic correspondence to the heavenly realm. Nor does it appear that we are simply importing a problem. Ideally, authority in primitive and archaic society would simply be assumed. But in Israel, authority was felt to be a problem. Erich Auerbach points out the conscious "claim to absolute authority" of biblical narrative.[35] Another area in which the authority question becomes explicit is in the treatment of the authority of the prophetic word. Was the true prophet the one who correctly predicted the future, the one who pronounced destruction or, conversely, salvation, the one who was properly installed in office, or the one who stood in the council of God and received a "call" and charisma? That no single adequate answer was found need not surprise us. A third example of the manifestation of the concern with authority is the significance of the "will of God" as pointed out by Henri Frankfort.[36] Talcott Parsons is more explicit when he says that in particular the law was seen in Israel as the revelation of the will of God and that this law acted as a fundamental normative order independent of all human political structures.[37] But the "will of God," freed from simple equation with "what is," becomes a high-level abstraction which it is difficult to apply at the practical level.

When the ontological grounding of authority and norms is thus put into question by the debunking perspective, how is the problem of authority handled by the society? The functional emphasis of experiential theology in which the perceptual shift is more directly linked with the expression in commitment and *action* than with the formulation of cognitive information offers one clue. Specifically, the question itself is changed from a focus on unchanging independent content norms (legitimating "what is"), which are prior to action, to a focus on the action demanded by the change of perception, the imperative contained in the promise. While the nature of the action demanded is important, it is directly linked to the shift in perception and not something added. Gregory Bateson also emphasizes the interaction of value, action, and perception.[38]

The second clue suggested by experiential theology is the emphasis on the *structures* as contrasted to a concern only with content. René Wellek and Austin Warren remark that our interpretation of a literary work of art involves the imposition on us by that work of norms which are neither unchanging principles nor completely subjectively derived and relative.[39] Similarly, the act of perception involves certain norms which our constructed reality imposes on us. The norm cannot be handled as an intervention from an ontologically transcendent realm, nor can the society retreat into extreme relativism and continue to function. Let us look at three types of authority in Israel: the authority of experience, the authority of universalism, and the authority of the intrinsic norm.

A
The Authority of Experience
Amos Wilder speaks of Jesus as a charismatic, "the seer with visionary sensibility and at the same time the clear-headed realist. He sees the connection of prodigious matters in the twinkling of an eye and can crystallize such vision in a parable or metaphor of the utmost simplicity."[40] Ultimately it is the new vision of the prophet, his perceptual shift, which is the source of

his authority, however this vision may be interpreted and talked about. Seen from the perspective of experiential theology, the prophetic call narratives appear to thematize this shift of perception which sets off the so-called classical prophet with his charismatic authority from the prophet whose position in the institutional apparatus provides his primary legitimation. Of course, as Peter Berger has argued, the options of charisma and institution are not mutually exclusive.[41] Thus it may be that the position of the call narrative in Isaiah 1—39 (chapter 6) is not simply a redactional accident but may reflect the fact that Isaiah was a prophet (institutionally) before he became a prophet (i.e., experienced the perceptual shift). The prophetic call narrative kernelizes the prophet's message, which is an outworking of his perceptual shift. Its centrality as a genre of prophetic proclamation may be because it is particularly appropriate (1) to evoke a similar perceptual shift in the audience to whom the prophet's oracles are directed and (2) to guide the interpretation of this oracular proclamation by those who to some degree have experienced a similar restructuring.

Naturally the self-authenticating experience of the perceptual shift is not limited to the prophets. Rather, "the day shall come when I will pour out my spirit on all mankind; your sons and your daughters shall prophesy, your old men shall dream dreams and your young men see visions (Joel 2:28, NEB)." The vision creates for those who experience it a new world. This new world implies a different set of norms—or is a new set of norms, as here with Wellek and Warren we wish to avoid the dichotomies of form and content as well as those of action and knowledge.[42] This new vision cannot be "proved," although there is the possibility of providing the conditions in which others might undergo an analogous perceptual shift. At other times there can only be the "come and see" pointed out in chapter 2—the call for participation as in Psalm 46:9. Isaiah 53:1ff. is perhaps the best example of self-testimony to a radical perceptual shift in the Old Testament. Here is related the experience of those among whom the "servant" lived his life of suffering and rejection. They do not proclaim any "dogma," a correct theology of suffering to replace their previous inadequate theology. Rather, they testify in symbolic language to the totality of the shift which they have experienced at the pretheological and prereflective level and to its radical significance for their lives. Thus the "authority of experience" emphasizes testimony and commitment/action while deemphasizing cognitive statements of the norms.

B
The Authority of Universalism

Amos Wilder also speaks of the universalism of Jesus "as in his attitude to the Samaritans, his attitudes to nature and the creatures . . . ; his appeals to reason, common sense and the processes of nature."[43] What Wilder says here is evocative of what I wish to point out for Israel, perhaps less fully realized there at any one time and place: The prophetic use of language, the debunking of institutions which raise ontological claims, the direct access to experience seen in the wisdom literature, in the metaphors of the prophets, and in the motivation of the law (to be discussed) all point beyond culture and ideologically bound perspectives to an implicit universalism. *Any universalism involves, however, an implicit claim to authority and thus has normative character.* What is being said here can be usefully compared with the "negative hermeneutic" (chapters 3 and 6) which attempts to establish an element of continuity in basic human conflicts and to transcultural symbols such as the parable. The implicit nature of the claim is to be emphasized. The parable does not start with a deductive assumption about the nature of man but rather with a particular experience. To the extent that this experience is translated into a dogma about man, and the implicit universalism is transformed into an explicit universalism, the danger of reification surfaces once again.

It is, of course, the freeing from a reified objectification of any particular political or social order which opens the way in Israel to an implicit universalism. We are faced with a paradox. The ancient Near Eastern world view, while explicitly universalistic, is ultimately revealed to be most particularistic and ideological. A radical relativism, by its appeal to human experience as such, turns out to be implicitly universalistic to the extent that the "man" addressed is seen primarily in his humanity rather than in his typicalization of particular roles. Thus what Wilder and Auerbach refer to as biblical realism and holism—the emphasis on all aspects of human experience—contributes to the authority of universalism.

Implicit universalism in the Old Testament may be linked up with our earlier discussion of biblical narrative and history. The discussion of Edwin Muir on the novel is extremely useful at this point. Muir discusses three major types of novels: character novel, dramatic novel, and chronicle. Only the first two concern us here. The character novel concentrates on space and existence, on the portrayal of a slice of the social world, its characters being "flat" and without development. The imaginative world of the dramatic novel is time and experience. Its stage is "the earth" rather than civilization.[44]

The complete range of human experience is portrayed in the action of the very particular characters of the dramatic novel. It is the turn to time and experience which I have discussed as characteristic of Old Testament narrative, while such a "novel" as Sinuhe would correspond more closely to the character novel. According to Muir, the work of art cannot make the universal its subject matter. Rather, the universal "can only be there when the particular is evoked." The "values of the character novel are social; *of the dramatic novel individual or universal as we choose to regard them.*"[45] Thus the turn to the particularism of the "dramatic novel" or its analogue in the Old Testament implies a universalism behind the particular which, unlike the character novel, is not limited to any one culture or civilization as its "stage."

Let us look at several examples of implicit universalism in the Old Testament. Much discussion has centered around the source of the norms according to which Amos condemns the surrounding nations. It would seem that there is neither an inappropriate explicit application of Israel's laws to other nations nor a drawing from a well-defined and formulated concept of moral law generally recognized by the ancient Near Eastern world. Rather, the denial of the ultimate ontological grounding of the more superficial and explicit norms of the society allows the underlying universals to link up directly with life experience. It seems that we have a working out at the surface level of the authority of an implicit universalism based in experience which Amos probably would not himself have been able to formulate explicitly. It is characteristic of many implicit universals—such as the universals of grammar (and more obviously the rules of a particular grammar)—that, while they exercise control over a person, he is not necessarily able to state fully the particular universal. These implicit universals appear to come close to what is often called "common sense"—but only that common sense which is truly open to experience rather than being based on a petrified ("it has always been done this way") or mythical norm.

Talcott Parsons links the explicit universalistic concern of Israel (as found, for example, in Isaiah 40—55) with the renunciation of the right to political autonomy after the fall of Jerusalem in 587 B.C. He concludes that the result was the conception of a divinely controlled moral order which was independent of any specific social or political organization.[46] This explicit universalism with which Parsons deals is rooted in an implicit universalism which goes back long before the exile and is manifested in the election theology which involves the relationship of three parties (God, Israel, and those from whom Israel is elected) rather than just God and Israel (as in covenantal theology). We have referred earlier to the development of this election theology by the Yahwist. The clearest example of its implicit universalism is the statement to Abraham in Genesis 12:3 (KJV), that "in thee all families of the earth be blessed."

Third, we should note the positive role of foreigners in the Old Testament, as for example the role of the Phoenician woman in the opening of the Elijah cycle (1 Kings 17), of the Syrian Naaman in the Elisha cycle (2 Kings 5), and of Naomi, the mother of Ruth. Finally, the generalizing tendency evident in the decalogue is another example of implicit universalism. The last four commandments are extremely broad while their earlier forms were much more specific. An example of an earlier stage would be "thou shall not kidnap an Israelite man."[47] This generalizing of the "social" commandments combines with the a-metaphysical thrust of the first four commandments with their denial of other gods, images, and magical use of the divine name, and the emphasis of the sabbath as a religious day not based on the annual nature cycle and its mythological conception of time. The authority of universalism is thus rooted both in the negative debunking tendency and in the positive emphasis on experience.

C
The Authority of the Intrinsic Norm

Israel comes into existence in a world with an explicit concept of norm which held a crucial position in the total world view. The terms *maat* in Egyptian and *me* in Mesopotamian are variously translated but refer basically to a world order which was established at the beginning and which finds manifestation in the order of the cosmos, in the political and social order, and in the natural order.[48] The usages of these two terms are perhaps the most vivid demonstration of the grounding of the societal and cultural systems of the ancient Near East in a massive and explicit ontology. What does Israel do with and to this norm concept? In the pre-Israelite usage, two Hebrew words, *šlm* (traditionally "peace," "wholeness") and *ṣdqh* (traditionally "justice," "righteousness"), function much the same as *maat* and *me* in Egypt and Mesopotamia. What is significant, then, is what happens to the usage over a period of time and in certain circles which freed themselves from the archaic ontologies. Walter Eisenbeis in a recent study concludes that *šlm* refers to a norm concept which occupies a central role in the Old Testament. Among the nonclassical prophets the word is linked to an archaic ontology. However, Eisenbeis argues, the classical prophets freed it from its ontological roots and gave it a dynamic character.[49] His study demonstrates how difficult it is to link this dynamic usage of the classical prophets to any specific content apart from its realization in a particular historical situation. Hans Schmid's recent study of *ṣdqh* similarly points toward a grounding in an archaic ontology. He argues that Israelite usage differs significantly from Canaanite usage. What is involved is again an uprooting of the word from its basis in an archaic ontology, the imbuing of it with a dynamic quality in which what is *ṣdqh* has to be determined in each specific instance. Thus in Israel, although the locus of the norm cannot be pinpointed in any referential or ontological realm, the concept of a norm continues to function.

The emphasis does not fall on specific and unchanging content but rather is dynamically determined as the action called for in the specific situation. Thus the concept of the intrinsic norm.

To speak of the intrinsic norm indicates the relationship to the situation to which it applies. Eric D. Hirsch similarly uses the phrase "intrinsic genre," emphasizing that the genre must be determined—in a rather inductive fashion—for each text. No fully worked out system of genres can be deductively built a priori into which individual texts are then categorized. One might well address the question of what is the "mode of existence" of such an intrinsic norm, just as Wellek and Warren address the same question to the mode of existence of the system of norms intrinsic to a literary work of art.[50] Their response that there is no need to reify this system of norms nor, on the other hand, to give in to a complete relativism or subjectivism seems equally appropriate to the approach of experiential theology and to the treatment of the norm in at least some segments of ancient Israel. Just as there are right and wrong interpretations, so there are right and wrong actions. The mode of existence of the norms is neither physical, nor mental, nor ideal.[51] The mode of existence is analogous to the mode of existence of the language system (langue) and its norms, which is concretized only partially in individual actions of speech (parole). Further, it can be compared to the mode of existence of the "model" which the structural anthropologist finds operating beneath and generating the surface forms of social structure and norms in a society.[52] While an idealist and ontological viewpoint on norm is rejected, this does not lead necessarily to a teleological conceptualization of the norm. The very ability to live with such a nonspecific understanding of the norm shows the same tolerance of complexity emphasized elsewhere in this volume as characteristic of creative religious growth.

Undoubtedly there was much outright bad action on the part of the Israelites which would be condemned by the prophets as contrary to the will of God and by much of mankind anywhere. The authority of experience as well as the authority of implicit universalism would seem to provide the basis for such prophetic condemnation. But the "will of God," although seemingly a concrete expression of the locus of norms in Israel, often turns out to be very nebulous to specify. "He has showed you, O man, what is good; and what does the Lord require of you but to do justice, and to love kindness, and to walk humbly with your God? (Mic.6:8)." How very clear in some situations and yet how very elusive in others. The will of God is a normative concept—thus denying extreme relativism—and yet a dynamic concept oriented to action and subject to change.

Certainly the "law" was regarded as one important manifestation of the will of God in the Old Testament. Yet the intrinsic and dynamic element of this law should not be overlooked. First, we note Erhard Gerstenberger's contention that the law which is most characteristic of Israel—apodictic law (e.g., "thou shalt not" statements)—originates in the clan ethos and is thus intimately connected with experience.[53] Second, we recall the presence of several large corpuses of law in the Old Testament, including the Book of the Covenant (Exodus 21—23), the Deuteronomic code (Deuteronomy 12—25), and the Holiness code (Leviticus 17—26). Here is revealed the ability of Israelite law to change and adapt to new conditions. Each code claims to be the revelation of the will of God, and yet their coexistence testifies to the refusal to reify any particular (and inevitably inadequate) manifestation of that will. Third, we have the decalogue and other short series of laws. The decalogue functions as a kernelization of the larger corpus of laws. This leaves the individual laws in the larger corpus free to change and allows for considerable leeway in their application. Here is a norm within the norm, analogous to a canon within the canon. Fourth, within the decalogue we find, as Norbert Lohfink has shown, that one specific commandment is given particular emphasis and functions as the "chief commandment."[54] At one time it may be the "no other gods," at another the "no image," and at still another time the sabbath commandment. Thus in the law we have the manifestation of an intrinsic norm whose specific manifestation at various levels is dynamic and subject to change. The experience-oriented nature of Old Testament law can further be seen in the presence of motivation clauses which state a reason why someone should obey the law (e.g., "so that your days may be long in the land" or "because you were slaves in Egypt"). As

Berend Gemser pointed out, such motivation clauses, almost entirely absent in other ancient Near Eastern law codes, become progressively more frequent in Israelite laws.[55]

Let us stand back and approach the problem of norm and authority from a slightly different perspective, using some insights of structuralism.[56] *My basic thesis is that the deep structure is the intrinsic norm behind the explicit norm.* The deep structure, as noted earlier, is not a matter of explicit content but rather unites form and content. The deep structure is never directly manifested at the surface. Conscious models and norms, while depending upon the deep structure, often hide rather than reveal that deep structure.[57] It is these conscious norms, legitimated by the mythologies, which are relativized by the debunking orientation. Thus the way is opened to a more immediate mediation of the deep structure at the surface, as may happen in the case of implicit universals and intrinsic norms.

A problem remains, however. It would be expected that when one group of surface norms is discredited, another will take its place. Does anything then change significantly? In response, we note that some surface norms may participate in a dynamic form-content hierarchy in which the "form" at one level becomes the content to a form at the next higher level.[58] This form-content hierarchy may help avoid the danger of reification by shifting the emphasis away from any unchanging, ontologically based norms. Such a form-content hierarchy is manifested in many fields, of which we will note three examples. (1) A simple literary genre (form) may become part of the content out of which a more complex genre is constructed. (2) In our earlier discussion of levels of law, each lower level was both content to the next higher level and form to the next lower level. For example, a decalogue would be form to a more extensive and particularistic law code and content to a more general fundamental commandment such as the "kelals" of Jewish tradition (e.g., the golden rule).[59] (3) The development of the term Torah in the Old Testament from instruction given orally by the priest to ultimately include the whole Pentateuch with its normative narrative again exemplifies how what is form at one (in this case historical) stage becomes content for the next stage.[60] Obviously the form-content hierarchy is in no way unique to Israel. However, we may suggest that one result of the debunking tendency in Israel is that even the norm at the "top" of the hierarchy is relativized and subject to change.[61]

While this allows for a dynamic function of norms at the surface level, how do we avoid either a complete relativism (or external determinism) or an innatism (Chomsky) which sees no fundamental change? Jean Piaget proposes "constructionism" as a third possibility. According to Piaget, the intrinsic norm or structure itself is changing and subject to growth in a spiral fashion, with one stage providing the basis on which the next stage is constructed.[62] As the structure at any one point still controls the surface manifestations, this does not lead to relativism.

This is an admittedly speculative treatment of the locus and function of authority and norm in Israel. To recapitulate, my resulting model is: (1) the surface phenomena, (2) the fundamental (explicit) norm and near-kernel formulations, and (3) the deep-level (intrinsic) norm with its constructed and changing character. This model has interesting possibilities for the treatment of a number of Old Testament problems such as the relation of the kernel oracle (chapter 4) to the fuller statement; the relation of the postulated amphictyonic model (sacral tribal league) to actual political organization in the period of the judges; the date of the formulation of brief historical credos (e.g., Deuteronomy 26:5-9) and their relationship to the basic narrative outline of Genesis through Joshua; and the date of crystallization of tradition complexes such as "Zion." My suggestion is that in some cases the model, kernel, or norm may be implicit in the deep-level structure and only subsequently—if ever (the amphictyony never becomes explicit in preserved texts)—is made explicit as in the credo. Even if there is no "time lag," the relationship between basic surface phenomena, explicit fundamental norms (or the functional equivalent), and the deep-level norm is more complex than mere identity (allowing for condensation). Thus, for example, the incongruity between actual political life and the amphictyonic model is not conclusive evidence against the functioning of an amphictyonic model at either surface or deep levels.[63]

The crystallization of the intrinsic norm into a related funda-mental norm or near-kernel formulation may be either func-tional or disfunctional, as it facilitates the processes of growth and tolerance of complexity or acts in an opposite direction, especially as the result of subsequent reification. The more general the explicit norm, the greater is its intrinsic claim to authority, the more functional and less content-oriented it is in application, and hence the less subject to reification.

In summary: the Old Testament exhibits a debunking thrust which is directed against all reifications of humanly constructed realities. This thrust is linked with the turn from myth to history (a diachronic structuring of reality) as the primary means of self-understanding, a perceptual shift rooted in a particular constellation of historical circumstances. This does not mean that synchronic structuring ceases. Israel must live with both the first fruits of the new way of perceiving as well as with the remnants of the old way. This introduces additional tension and the seeds of further change.[64] One area in which such tension is manifested is that of authority and norms, leading to the development of a more functional and less content-centered conception of authority.

Naturally the danger existed that Israel's debunking tendency with its related handling of the problem of authority could be transformed into a reified ideology. This danger became es-pecially great when the set of historical circumstances which gave rise to the debunking style dissolved and gave way to a different set of circumstances (i.e., a new historical paradigm). The movement from the preexilic Old Testament situation to the New Testament situation is a movement from one historical paradigm to its successor (as briefly mentioned at the end of chapter 4). Thus it is necessary to ask how the Old Testament's debunking tendency and its conception of authority was under-stood (or misunderstood), continued, transformed, or aban-doned in the New Testament and early church. The answer to this question will have obvious implications for the treatment of the relationship between the Testaments and for the contempo-rary hermeneutical task.

If the discussion of experiential theology elsewhere in this volume is correct in its analysis of the growth experience evoked by Jesus' challenge, this and the preceding chapter may illustrate and help explain the genesis of the experiential thrust of the Bible. In examining the Old Testament some now-familiar themes appeared—openness to experience, heightening of conflict, a-metaphysical use of language, dereification of institutions and ideologies—as well as some common problems, especially concerning authority and norms for action. Further examination of the dynamics of religious experience generally may provide additional insight into the religious experience of ancient Israel, especially in evaluating what is and is not fundamental to the understanding of this experience. Sorting this out would seem to be a priority task for Old Testament theology today.

experienced jesus and christ event: hermeneutical reflections

J. CHRISTIAAN BEKER

In chapter 1 I suggested the need for a return from biblical theology to biblical religion. The possibility of such a return clearly depends on the viability of a new hermeneutical approach.

The experiential theology developed in the intervening chapters reinforces my former suggestion and opens the way for such a new hermeneutic. The outline of the relationship between language and experience in Part Two and the articulation of the basic debunking attitude of the Old Testament prophets developed in the last two chapters opens up the possibility of a new biblical hermeneutic.

The basic a-metaphysical attitude of the Old Testament suggests as well the intrinsic importance of the Old Testament for understanding the New Testament. Leo Baeck's dictum seems reinforced within a hermeneutical context: The New Testament without the Old Testament is Gnosticism.

The question remains, however, to what extent the basic Old Testament insights into religious perception can be applied to the New Testament. Crucial difficulties obtain both because the implicit norms of authority in the Old Testament seem to have become very explicit in the New Testament and because the given world view in the New Testament seems so much more normative and determinative than the Old Testament critique on the world view of its neighbors. The New Testament seems to have absorbed the apocalyptic world view within its religious categories. "Apocalypticism was the reaction at the literary level to the metaphysical orientation of Greek thought. . . . Thus we may regard apocalypticism as a transformation of history and eschatology, a sort of narrated eschatology with a literalized and ontologized use of the old mythic language (see chapter 5, page 138). The apocalyptic world view now determines the language of New Testament religion and constitutes its basic interpretative framework. And since apocalypticism has intrinsic speculative character, it propels thought away from living experience to metaphysical structures which in turn dictate to man's experience and imprison it. The problem is whether New Testament religion stands or falls with its apocalyptic expression—whether debunking or demythologizing can succeed in liberating the husk from the core—whether the apocalyptic world view is not only the linguistic expression of New Testament experience but also its determinant.

Succinctly, we face the question of the apple core or the onion. Will demythologizing yield an experiential core *for us* behind the husk or will it finally stare at nothing among a heap of discarded onion peels?

Connected with the ontologized structure of apocalypticism is the question of authority. For within an apocalyptic mind set, religious authority is bound up with ontological realities which have an independent supernatural existence. There seems nothing *implicit* in the New Testament about the authoritative norm; every ethical and theological assertion circles around the once and for all of Jesus Christ as God's final self-revelation. "Every spirit which confesses that Jesus Christ has come in the flesh is of God, and every spirit which does not confess Jesus is not of God (1 John 4:2-3a)."

In the light of these obstacles—the apocalyptic world view and the positing of an explicit authority as the final determinant in all historical-religious questions—the conditions for the development of a viable New Testament hermeneutic seem highly dubious.

The attempted answer to the hermeneutical problem we will call a hermeneutic of experience. Such a hermeneutic of experience, it will be suggested, attempts to uncover the fundamental religious experience which the biblical authors evoke. This religious experience, expressed in a theologically culturally conditioned language, allows an insight into the factors which gave rise to it and raises hope for subsequently transcultural relevance to occur. In what follows we will discuss a hermeneutic of experience along the following lines:

I. Introduction to a hermeneutic of experience
  A. The viability of a hermeneutic of experience
    1. The authority of experience
    2. Experience and world view
  B. The character of a hermeneutic of experience
II. A hermeneutic of experience in practice
  A. The resurrection in the New Testament, with special attention to Paul
  B. The religious meaning of the resurrection for Paul

I

INTRODUCTION TO A
HERMENEUTIC OF EXPERIENCE

A
The Viability of a Hermeneutic of Experience

1. The authority of experience. A key hermeneutical question is the authority of the Bible. A hermeneutic of experience locates this authority neither in its language nor in any ontological reality. Thus it rests the authority of the Bible not in its unique conceptuality—not in its God-given inspired language —and not in any Word or kerygma which lies as an ontological reality behind the language, that is, in *"die Sache"* behind the words.

A hermeneutic of experience insists that biblical authority lies in *a fundamental religious experience* which the biblical authors *evoke,* in a new perspective on reality which is reflected in their language. Normally the authority of the New Testament is located in the Christ-event. This highly formal answer leaves the decisive question unanswered. For what *is* the meaning of the Christ-event? Usually the following options are presented:

a. The Christ-event is an *ontological* reality which inserts itself into our world of *felt experience* without a clear referent to that world of experience.

b. The Christ-event is a unique historical event, a divine "fact" which forms the decisive part of a divine strategy of salvation. As such it should determine all our faith and action (e.g., Oscar Cullmann).

c. The Christ-event is an existential event which cannot be verified historically, but can only be appropriated through the preaching of "the kerygma" (e.g., Rudolf Bultmann).

d. The Christ-event is a language event; the creative language of the kerygma creates in the hearer the new experience of being in Christ (e.g., the New Hermeneutic).

All these formulations have two common features which are mutually related. They all have an ontological referent—the Christ-event is a "supernatural something"—and they stress the discontinuity between the reality of the Christ-event and the world of our ordinary experience. In other words, the language, whether metaphysical or existential, functions to assert a specific interpretation of the discontinuity of the Christ-event within the continuum of human experience. *Indeed, the "ontological" description of the Christ-event seems a necessity in order to guarantee the discontinuity of the Christ-event.* The danger of a language focusing on experience is that it seems to accommodate the Christ-event within the sphere of our world of experience, so that the Christ-event derives from our experience rather than dictates to it. If the Christ-event becomes only a component of ordinary experience, the very "newness" which is normative for the Christ-event in the New Testament is destroyed and a hermeneutic of accommodation results rather than a hermeneutic which does justice to the New Testament. Brevard Childs expresses a widespread opinion when he writes in the context of a discussion of the relation of the biblical witness to the extrabiblical:

There are two classical reactions to the problem which can be readily dismissed. The first refuses to admit any real validity to a religious assertion outside the Bible. This position would argue that the Biblical writers did make use of common material, but they so transformed it as to sever any lines of continuity. The second classical response represents the other extreme. The Biblical witness can claim no special prerogatives to divine truth. The Bible represents one expression of human experience that must be related on the same level with all other human responses to the religious dimensions of life. The first alternative protects the uniqueness of the Bible by making it irrelevant to all general areas of human experience. *The second seeks for relevance by reducing the Biblical witness to the lowest common denominator.* In our opinion, neither of these two solutions is helpful.[1]

Childs's dismissal of the second alternative is not well founded; it implies that discontinuity must be bought with ontological language! In fact, the Christ-event suddenly becomes a conceptual content, alien to my experience—a proposition which is subsequently existentially packaged to avoid and undo the vacuum which it creates within my field of experience. The Christ-event in this case illustrates the peculiar reversal between experience and conceptuality. The concept operates as an entity *in se* and *per se*, an entity with a life substance of its own. Thus the conceptuality is no longer recognized as a linguistic tool which articulates and organizes my experience, but acquires absolutistic and ideological pretensions. It now becomes a substance which supposedly creates experience, but which in fact operates as a magic formula. The conceptuality now creates experience *ex opere operato* (on the basis of the performed work); language ceases to be a sacramental symbol but becomes a referent to sacramental *substance*. The Christ-event then becomes analogous to the Torah in first-century Judaism; it must be obeyed, simply because it *is;* it is a heavenly reality, on account of which and after which the world was created, so that a Jew is not allowed to question its *rationale* but must simply obey. Obedience to biblical authority thus threatens to degenerate into blind obedience and becomes oppressive and dehumanizing. Obedience loses its relation to insight; the obedience of discipleship is displaced by the obedience of slavery.

What is even more disastrous is the religious confusion which such a conception of the Christ-event brings about. Most Christians educated within a long-standing metaphysical Christian dogmatic tradition now invest the language with ultimate religious significance, because they consider the language to be the equivalent of the religious reality they honor. Thus they experience a confusion between their fundamental experience and the religious language; a "sacred language" controls the experience rather than the reverse.

In this scheme religious language is equated with descriptive-referential language. The language is reified so that it points to substances and objects of the supernatural world as if the world of religious objects is the empirical world of things in a supernatural dimension. This reversal of language and experience not only confuses Christians in the church but also blocks the way of religious inquirers. How can they honestly satisfy a longing for religious experience at the cost of sacrificing their intellectual honesty? Do ultimate questions of seriousness in my life depend on an ultimate price, i.e., my personal integrity?

This reversal of language and experience is at first glance not a deliberate perversion of New Testament religiosity. Rather it seems to have been facilitated and promoted by the metaphysical tendencies of New Testament apocalyptic language. That language supports a speculative interpretation, because it is both referential and reifying language locating the focus of religious perception in a heavenly topography and in supernatural objects. The question, then, of the authority of the New Testament and especially that of the Christ-event cannot be solved apart from a consideration of the apocalyptic world view. The critical question arises as to the adequacy of apocalyptic language within the New Testament itself to communicate the experience evoked by the historical Jesus. Is the apocalyptic world view and its language a pathological distortion of Jesus' intention or not?

We will address ourselves to the issue of the apocalyptic world view later. Our attention now focuses on the discontinuity question as the correlate of the authority problem. A hermeneutic of experience asserts that Christian experience is discontinuous experience, without having to posit a metaphysical realm. The complaint against a hermeneutic of experience is that the language of experience reduces the revelation of God to a religious humanism; it subjectifies the objective language of revelation and thus fails to do justice to the priority of God and the objective reality of the "facts" of God in salvation history in the witness of the biblical writers. Consequently, it abrogates the uniqueness of the Bible and its authority and encapsulates the Bible within the categories of human experience. Particularly the language of experience is under attack; it is essentially reductionistic because it cannot do justice to the discontinuity which is so characteristic of the Christ-event, and thus it accommodates the biblical witness to the level of general human experience. The Christ-event becomes a derivative of human experience and not the totally new experience which "no eye has seen, nor ear heard, nor the heart of man conceived (1 Cor. 2:9)." Succinctly: human spirit is illegitimately mixed with the Holy Spirit of God.

The basic assumption behind statements like these is erroneous, namely, that human experience is constricted to a worldly continuum which cannot adopt elements discontinuous with its former field of experience. If it is objected that the new elements of experience which man adopts are nevertheless not "uniquely" new but only "relatively" new, I can only respond that experience is fundamentally all that man has and that distinctions between relatively new and uniquely new are a meaningless retreat to an ontological language game, apart from the fact that an outsider can never prescribe an experience as relatively new to the experiencer who himself experiences it as radically new. If someone wants to maintain that the Christ-event is a radically dualistic phenomenon which has no possible connections with man's field of experience and that man's experience runs on a radically monistic continuum, he must interpret the New Testament Christ-event in a Gnostic-dualistic manner and separate the Creator from the Redeemer in such a way that the experience of redemption can only be apprehended by a superhuman man who has no more contact in any sense with the created man which he was before—a man into whom a new nature has been infused. Man's Gnostic self-apotheosis is the result of a radical dichotomy between his status as a human "experiencer" and as an alleged "superhuman" experiencer. In this way experience becomes the dehistoricizer of man; man loses hold of himself as a *historical* creature and zooms off in some divine sphere, whether ecstatically or psychedelically. (It is one of the great merits of Rudolf

Bultmann to have detected that the Gnostic imagery of the New Testament was interpreted by the New Testament authors in a profound historical sense.)

   2. Experience and world view. A hermeneutic of experience insists that in some way it is necessary to penetrate behind the biblical language to the experience which the language attempts to express. An oversimplified version of this problem would say: A hermeneutic of experience searches for an *abiding experience* within the discontinuity of world views, something Harry Emerson Fosdick already formulated. Unless it is possible to express in terms of our world view the experience which the biblical authors evoked for their time, the Bible remains either a closed book for us or compels us to live in a for us outdated and archaic world view. The usual hermeneutical distinction between *Sprachgestalt* (language form) and *Sachverhalt* (material content) is misleading because it assumes a continuity of *Sache* (subject matter) across the discontinuity of world views. A hermeneutic of experience suspects the metaphysical implications of *"die Sache"* whether conceived as *the* kerygma or *the* Word.

   However, the search for an "abiding experience" is no solution to the problem, since it is at closer inspection both naïve and irrelevant. It is naïve because it overlooks the interrelation between world view and experience. It overlooks the fact that language actively shapes our experience. To be sure, experience expresses itself in language, but language also determines our experience. The phrase "an abiding experience" thus naïvely assumes that there is a package of nonlinguistic experience which floats through the ages.

   The positing of an abiding experience is irrelevant as well, since one cannot gain access to the pure experience of someone else. That experience always reaches one within the language of the experiencer's world view. In the first place, the content of someone else's experience is uniquely his own; it is basically private. In the second place, if communication of the experience takes place, it occurs always within the language system of the experiencer's world view. It would be fallacious for a hermeneutic of experience to distill a package of biblical experiences and apply it to the problems of our time, because the content of biblical experiences are the product of problems in biblical times out of which the experiences evolve. An "abiding experience" is a misleading goal, because it ignores the insight of the sociology of knowledge in the mutual interaction of language and experience, the insight that language not only expresses experience but shapes and determines it.

We need to take a step back and reflect here on the complex relationship between experience and world view, as is apparent in any discussion of ideology. There are times when ideology so dominates the culture that it actively shapes all our experiences and feelings. The absolutist pretensions of ideology become clear when we ask: Why do people make absolute claims for their world view rather than realize its essential relativity? Why do culturally conditioned definitions of reality achieve the status of *the* objectively true reality of things? Once I have become aware of the culturally conditioned world view of the New Testament and likewise of the relativity of my own, I must despair of the question of *the* true world view—a world view which corresponds to the objective truth of the nature of reality. The sociology of knowledge makes me aware of an important truth, my inability to define "the ultimate truth"; it forces me to turn my back on metaphysical questions and constrains me to come to terms with my own experience. Thus that world view is true for me which most adequately articulates my life experience for me, i.e., which *functions* adequately in my life.

The sociology of knowledge leads me to a pragmatic definition of truth in the tradition of the pragmatic philosophy of William James. Once I recognize the need for a world view as the articulation of my experience, I am able to recognize as well the way in which my experiences and their articulations are bound by the ideology of my culture. The culture in which I live is, as it were, the ideological super-ego, which in a variety of ways governs and delimits my experience and its linguistic articulation. For instance, in a culture for which achievement is the ideal, it must be exceedingly difficult to understand the New Testament emphasis on faith and grace in any other way than within a context of achievement. Here *works* of faith and sanctification as the *fruit* of grace become the predominant interpretations of faith and grace. Thus the New Testament language of faith and grace is subsumed under the ideological language of the culture and is hardly able to break the "achievement" assumption of that culture. The greater the cultural distance—the greater the alien character of another culture—the more difficult empathy becomes. Yet the greater the empathy with an alien culture, the more my ability to uncover the ideological assumptions of my own culture.

Too often an alien text (such as a first-century New Testament text) operates on a twentieth-century reader in much the same way as an alien culture operates on an American tourist: everything which does not fit his "American way of life" is regarded as a cute curiosity or is rejected as a "primitive" stage, and usually the best things he finds in an alien culture are a Hilton Hotel, a hamburger, a cola, and fellow American tourists; that is, items which fit the experiences of his own culture. In other words, the natural attitude of man is not only to express his experiences in terms of his own culture and world view but also to let his world view determine his experiences. Ideology determines us so consciously and subconsciously that our way of life becomes *the* universal way of life.

There are times, however, when new experiences crack open the current ideological system. Once I discover the conflict between my own experience of life and that of my culture, I experience acute disorientation. So the revolutionary mood is born, necessitating a fundamental reorientation and with it a search for a new "language" over against the language of the dominant culture, "the establishment." Revolution occurs when cultural speech structures and the experiences they articulate (one's habitual world view) no longer express felt experience. Experience then must find a new language appropriate to it. In such a situation violent reactions occur; if the experience cannot find adequate expression, it escapes into forms of mystic silence, ecstatic utterance, or violent action. Usually the dominant world view is so strong that the experience is either suffocated or domesticated and reroutinized within the given world view.

After these general observations, we can put the basic question for a hermeneutic of experience concisely: *If language actively shapes our experience and if experience itself is a private experience which cannot be captured apart from linguistic expression—in other words, if we have no access to experience apart from language—is not a hermeneutic of experience caught between two mutually exclusive poles and thus reduced to silence?* In terms of the New Testament, if the apocalyptic world view is alien to us and if we are forced to reach behind it to the experience which expresses itself in apocalyptic categories, but if at the same time we cannot gain access to the experience apart from apocalyptic language which itself has shaped the experience, what else is there to do but acknowledge that the biblical experience is lost to us forever and that no experiential bridge can be constructed between the experience of biblical men and our own?

Indeed, a hermeneutic of experience recognizes the insight of the sociology of knowledge, namely, that there is a radical discontinuity between different world views and that a particular world view shapes the experience of its adherents. However, it insists that this valuable insight cannot overlook the "commonality" of "the body," the fact that there is an existential continuum in all human life which gives rise to common problems notwithstanding the discontinuity of cultures and world views; this commonality of problems is the essential foundation for a hermeneutic of experience. For how else can the New Testament Gospel become a gospel for *us?* As Batson has pointed out in his cone diagram (chapter 3), the issue is not a positing of universal problems throughout the total range of human experience. Rather, a careful distinction must be made between the particular problems of a given culture and genuinely universal human problems. However, unless there are such genuine universals, biblical interpretation will be caught in exploring problems too specific and too culture-bound as to be hermeneutically helpful to elucidate human experience in the present. Whether such genuine universals actually exist is an open problem. Without them, however, no hermeneutical solution is in sight. The basic question is whether the extreme particularity of human experience is not corroded and annulled when raised to the level of universal abstractions. On this point more precision is necessary.

B
The Character of a Hermeneutic of Experience

Is there then any transcultural power to the New Testament experience? What are the conditions for a hermeneutic of experience over against our usual hermeneutic of updating or accommodation—a hermeneutic engaged in salvage operations which becloud the real issues? Far too often the ministry of the church confuses *interpretatio* (hermeneutics) with *applicatio* (homiletical concreteness). In this way hermeneutics is reduced to ad hominem appeals and persuasions, whereas the metaphysical assumptions behind the *applicatio* are tacitly assumed: for example, "Of course, Christ rose from the dead. But the important thing is whether you live a new life."

At this point a hermeneutic of experience posits four fundamental assertions with respect to the complex relation between language and experience. I prefer to call them the four pillars of a hermeneutic of experience. The model of the experience-language-experience process of Christian re-creation presented in chapter 3 provides the basis for this discussion.

1. A three-story linguistic universe can clarify the relation between language and experience.

> a. The experience itself, essentially prelinguistic and preconceptual.
>
> b. The linguistic expression of the experience, i.e., the level of symbolic religious language as primary form of language. Here attention is focused on its symbolic character, its openness to the experience which it expresses.
>
> c. Theological-interpretative language, in which the symbolic religious language is taken into the mainstream of the established ideology of the culture and interwoven with its structures of meaning. A hardening of language has taken place, a further conceptualization. Attention focuses on the meaning of the language rather than on the experience which originally shaped the linguistic expression.

2. A hermeneutic of experience insists that the *function* of symbolic religious language is toward action-commitment

rather than toward understanding. As suggested in chapter 2. the question evoked by symbolic religious language is more "What shall I do?" than "What does it mean?" In other words, what is at stake in the difference between theological language and religious language is the difference between an appeal to the intellect and appeal to total commitment.

3. The commitment question of symbolic religious language is not just an appeal to man's moral nature but to a new perception of reality as the motivating power behind man's new posture toward reality.

At this point the contribution of existentialist phenomenology, especially the phenomenology of perception by Merleau-Ponty outlined in chapter 2, should be clear. Its stress on primordial perception over against the "natural attitude" of man, on the nonlogical perceptual shift involved in a figure-ground reversal as developed by Gestalt psychologists, enables the New Testament interpreter to give an account of "disclosure" situations which the Bible calls "revelation." Existentialist phenomenology may overcome a view of experience which stresses the "natural" attitude as the continuum of man's experience in the world and allows for a radical shift in perception which is capable of being interpreted as the experience of the holy or of grace in terms of its character as unexpected surprise and sheer given-ness. Thus it may overcome a sterile subject-object dichotomy, since it binds together within one Gestalt the perceiver and the perceived. It accounts for the primordial character of experience in the life of men and allows a new perspective on the relation between experience and its linguistic expression. It allows for the unpacking of the New Testament language into its original experiential components in the life of the biblical witnesses.

4. A hermeneutic of experience insists that symbolic religious language can be unpacked in terms of its experiential components. But since the content of the experience is always either private or linguistically determined by one's world view, the goal of a hermeneutic of experience cannot be "an abiding experience," a transmissable content of experience. It must uncover the process of experience, i.e., the existential conflicts

which are the building blocks for the perceptual restructuring, for a new reality.

Whereas the perceptual shift—the revelatory moment—is private and not open to hermeneutical analysis, the elements which constitute the background material for the shift *and* their restructuring after the shift are open to public inspection. Thus a hermeneutic of experience is consciously a post-hoc analysis. A hermeneutic of experience asks: *Of what was the experience the result?* What gave rise to the experience as expressed in the language of a particular world view? Experience, then, in a religious context is a multifaceted term. It contains at least three elements: (a) a latent or open set of conflicts, (b) a new perception of these conflicts, and (c) a new direction and commitment as the enfleshment of the new perception.

Thus a hermeneutic of experience can only then "connect" with the language of the New Testament if it is possible to penetrate behind the world view and behind the religious language, to the conflictual elements which inform the perceptual shift.

A hermeneutic of experience consequently opposes a theological correlation scheme (Tillich). A "question-answer" model is erroneous because it suggests that the human situation provides the problems to which the Bible gives the answer. The Bible is not a problem-solving book in this sense; it does not give answers and solutions but provides a new direction. We might say: The Christ of the New Testament is not a problem solver but a redeemer; not *Auflöser* but *Erlöser.*

A hermeneutic of experience opposes an attempt to distill out of the New Testament a body of experiences which must answer man's perennial problems. Drawing upon the hermeneutical guidelines at the end of chapter 3, our hermeneutic of experience has two poles: negative and positive (cf. Batson, chapter 3). The *negative* hermeneutic attempts to unearth those basic existential conflicts in the biblical world which are not culturally created. These cross-cultural conflicts provide the basis for our existential participation and function in a way similar to Bultmann's preunderstanding. They have transcultural power. The biblical "solutions" to these conflicts are capable of giving us a direction but are themselves time-conditioned linguistic expressions which do not yield *answers* to us. This direction the Bible offers is the *positive* pole of the hermeneutic. Its positive aspect is conditional upon the transgressive power of the negative hermeneutic. Such a positive hermeneutic will attempt to probe the biblical language to the experience behind it. The norm for this positive *New Testament* hermeneutic can only be Jesus, who evokes a new perspective on man's basic conflicts. This hermeneutic concentrates not on the particular language and solutions which Jesus employed but on the particular direction into which he restructures man's basic conflicts.

The success or failure of a hermeneutic of experience, then, is conditioned by our ability to penetrate behind the *content* of the *New Testament language* and behind the *content* of the *New Testament experience* to the genuine human conflicts to which Jesus gave a specific direction.

In exegetical practice a hermeneutic of experience must be sensitive to the distinction between religious language and theological formulation. It must be sensitive to the possibility of unpacking not only the religious language but also its further theological conceptualization. The question is always: How does the language *function?* Is it basically open to the experience it meant to express, or is it "closure" language which cuts one off from the originating experience?

This is an exceedingly delicate task. For instance, how can we in the twentieth century, alienated from the apocalyptic world view, determine its function in the first century? Obviously the apocalyptic world view was a living and intensely felt expression of religious experience for a first-century apocalypticist. However, a hermeneutic of experience is mainly interested in the hermeneutical transcultural possibilities of the apocalyptic world view. And these hermeneutical possibilities seem severely limited. The apocalyptic interpretation of the Jesus-event seems to be "closure" language on two grounds: (a) it does not seem capable of being unpacked as to its originating source, the historical Jesus and the experience he evoked, and (b) it seems to give rise to metaphysical-speculative tendencies which posit heavenly realities and speculative schemes of history as determinative of experience rather than expressive of it.

Thus for twentieth-century man the apocalyptic world view is not only unintelligible but even intrinsically a "pathological" form of speech, an inadequate and misleading tool for the kind of religious experience it wanted to express.

The structural inadequacies of apocalyptic language should not blind us, however, to an element in it which is open to symbolic religious language and experience. That element is the feature of radical discontinuity between the old age and the new age so central to all apocalyptic thinking. This theological conceptuality is capable of being translated into experiential terms, for it expresses the radical shift in perceptual structures to which the Jesus-event gave rise.

II
A HERMENEUTIC OF
EXPERIENCE IN PRACTICE

It is especially Paul in the New Testament corpus who presents a test case for a hermeneutic of experience; he vividly illustrates the complex interaction between the various levels of the linguistic universe of a hermeneutic of experience. Paul seems to operate with a highly articulated theological conceptuality, and its openness to its experiential components often seems in doubt. For the central subject of Paul's theology—Jesus Christ—is resistant to the unpacking of its symbolic religious meaning. Paul's theological conceptuality is heavily influenced by his apocalyptic world view, and "Jesus Christ" seems a frozen concept because it is connected with the main apocalyptic event in Paul, the resurrection. The critical question thus becomes to what extent the resurrection of Jesus Christ is related to the person of Jesus and the experience he evoked. It may seem strange for a hermeneutic of experience with its heavy investment in the experienced Jesus to explore the Pauline letters and not the Synoptic Gospels. Paul is explored because of the critical question he raises for a hermeneutic of experience. As the earliest literary witness to the resurrection, he illustrates more than anyone else the amazing riddle of early Christianity, namely, that the resurrection event monopolized the scene to such an extent that no Jesus portraits survived. I will discuss the resurrection in the New Testament with special attention to Paul, and the religious meaning of the resurrection for Paul.

A
The Resurrection in the New Testament, with Special Attention to Paul

The resurrection is the central affirmation, not only of the New Testament but of Christian faith and theology. It has frequently been said that without the resurrection there would not have been Christianity: no church—no faith—no lordship of Jesus Christ. Thus theologians like Rudolf Bultmann and Hans Conzelmann regard the historical Jesus not as a theme for New Testament theology but as its presupposition: New Testament theology is only possible after Easter. Unless the resurrection is clarified, we have not dealt with the main issue of New Testament hermeneutics.

The central problem for a hermeneutic of experience is this: Is the resurrection experience of the disciples an experience which finds its expression within their particular world view but is itself not confined to that world view *or* are *both* the linguistic expression *and* the experience itself locked within a first-century world view, so as not to be transferable to a radically different world view?

A fundamentalist orientation will have no problem here. It will reject the discontinuity problem on the level of world view and therefore as well on the level of experience. For those Christians who acknowledge the discontinuity problem on the level of world view, the discontinuity problem on the level of experience must take two forms: Is the resurrection experience merely alien to my world view and thus a difficult but real possibility for my experience *or* is the resurrection experience not merely *alien to* my world view but also *alienated from* any experience possibility? The import of this statement is this: an *alien* text or experience constitutes a challenge to my experience; an *alienated* text or experience means that the challenge has been accepted and tried but to no avail; the experience in question seems so locked up within its own nexus of world view and experience that it fails to evoke my experience.

Some of the characteristic features of the resurrection experience as described in the New Testament are as follows:

1. 1 Corinthians 15 is the earliest and most reliable witness to the resurrection experience. The accounts in the Synoptics and John are not accounts of personal witnesses. Although they contain early material, they are so overlaid with legendary materials and apologetic motifs that they do not constitute an independent witness on the same level of reliability as Paul's.

2. The Synoptics and John accounts bring together two originally independent cycles of stories, namely, Empty Tomb stories centered around women and angelophanies and Appearance stories centered around disciples and Christophanies. Tradition history reveals a tendency toward localizing the resurrection in Jerusalem away from Galilee and toward shifting the "proof" of the resurrection from the Appearances to the Empty Tomb and to the disciples as now associated with the Empty Tomb and Jerusalem. The process culminates in Matthew and John, where a Christophany to the women takes place (Matthew 28) and where a Christophany occurs to Mary Magdalene at the Empty Tomb and where the disciples Peter and John come to faith purely on the evidence of the Empty Tomb (John 20).

3. The resurrection experience in Paul is part and parcel of a particular world view, namely, the apocalyptic world view of the New Testament, and is unintelligible apart from that world view. In other words, resurrection language can only be understood within the world view of which it is an integral part, the apocalyptic world view. Resurrection is not a category of Old Testament religion; it only appears at its periphery, at the time around the exile when the apocalyptic world view establishes itself via Parsistic influence into the Old Testament Jewish framework. Resurrection terminology within apocalypticism serves a double goal: a final theophany and a final theodicy. It expresses vindication for the faithful remnant in Israel which, contrary to its experience of persecution and death in the world, is now raised up and glorified by God as reward for its faithfulness. It expresses as well the manifestation of the kingdom of God—the New Age—which signals judgment and condemnation and destruction for Satan and his forces who have

ruled the Old Age. Both resurrection and the New Age express the miraculous new quality of life in the "other world," and they express it in dualistic, discontinuous fashion. God invades this evil world and breaks it off: the New Age and the resurrection are, within the apocalyptic world view, imminent and discontinuous realities; they are divine realities of complete bliss, peace, and vindication which will be manifested shortly. "Behold, the dwelling of God is with men. He will dwell with them, and they shall be his people, and God himself will be with them; he will wipe away every tear from their eyes, and death shall be no more, neither shall there be mourning nor crying nor pain any more, for the former things have passed away (Rev. 21:3-4)."

4. Within this apocalyptic ideology the resurrection of Jesus becomes quite intelligible. Paul indeed describes the resurrection experience with apocalyptic dimensions.

The resurrection is not cast as a resuscitation of a material body but as a visionary experience of the exalted Christ, clothed with a pneumatic body. The experience, in other words, is cast within the range and conceptuality of apocalyptic visions, the seeing of heavenly figures and a heavenly topography, as is the trademark of apocalyptic writers (see also Stephen in Acts 7:56).

The resurrection is not cast as an isolated miraculous occurrence in the midst of an ongoing history but as the apocalyptic prelude to the imminent end of history and the coming of the New Age. "But in fact Christ has been raised from the dead, *the first fruits* of those who have fallen asleep. . . . But each in his own order: Christ the first fruits . . . then comes the end (1 Cor. 15:20, 23-24; italics added)."

The meaning of the resurrection experience is determined by the eschaton, to which it is the prelude. The school of consistent eschatology is correct in pointing to the theological consequences of the Parousia delay (see the comments on Müller in chapter 5). This delay may mean the destruction of the apocalyptic world view as was soon to happen in Gnostic circles. It may bring about a structural difference in the experience of Christians with respect to the resurrection (cf 2 Peter). For what does resurrection mean in a context which is divorced from an imminent apocalyptic happening? In fact, the Lucan tradition minimizes the apocalyptic elements so clearly stressed by Paul, and thus in Luke the resurrection experience becomes a miracle in the midst of history—a proof of divine materialization on earth—and ceases to be the signal to the *temporal* end of our world and our history. For Luke the apocalyptic world view is not surrendered but pushed to the perimeter; the resurrection rather becomes the signal toward a *geographical* goal, the universal mission of the church in our history and world.

However, even apart from the imminence problem associated with the resurrection, what about the meaning of the resurrection of Christ once the apocalyptic world view of which it is a part collapses? Resurrection language then must function in a new "semantic environment": in Gnostic circles it becomes the equivalent of the heavenly-otherworldly pneumatic self dissociated from any contact with the material self (1 Corinthians 15; 2 Timothy 2:18), and in later Catholic Christianity it may become synonymous with the immortality of the soul; a privatized "post mortem" eschatology is substituted for the original cosmic eschatology.

Here is not the place to trace the history of the apocalyptic world view within Christianity. I suspect that once the crucial aspects of *imminence* in apocalypticism fall away, its pictorial images of the heavenly world—its images of hope—now become "an house of being": as noted in chapter 1, apocalypticism becomes the bridge between prophecy and speculative metaphysical theology. But this movement is already under way within the theology of Paul and the early church. Genuine debate is possible about the relation of prophecy and apocalypticism—about the genuine or contrived character of the apocalyptic writings. But whatever living pictorial or literary-ossified elements the apocalyptic world view exhibits, once the apocalyptic *image* is filled up with specific historical material *content,* it ceases to be an image and becomes a heavenly substance. Thus, when an actual historical person—Jesus—is transferred to the heavenly kingdom, the image of a Son of man is now displaced and reified by a heavenly substance, Jesus Christ as *the* Son of man.

Paul, then, not only expresses the resurrection experience of Jesus Christ within his apocalyptic world view, but this experience itself seems locked within that world view. Apart from the church as the body of Christ, there is now a new heavenly Christ body: the pneumatic body of Christ, which becomes the object of prayer and worship.

There seems to be no way of appropriating Paul's Christology without embracing his apocalyptic eschatology. The apocalyptic world view so dominates Paul's experience of Christ that the elimination of the world view eliminates the Christ-experience as well. One cannot demythologize the apocalyptic world view and retain a demythologized apocalyptic experience; both stand or fall together.

In fact, without vivid awareness of the apocalyptic-eschatological intensity of early Christian times we cannot understand Pauline Christianity. The consciousness of living in the last days—of occupying a stance on the abyss of history where the current of world history is about to reach a climax—has often been described. Yet the pulsating, all-encompassing power of the apocalyptic world view has not been sufficiently assessed. Too often it has been evaluated as "a framework" which could be either dispensed with or demythologized. After all, one reasoned, Christology did not fall away along with the apocalyptic world view in the history of the early Catholic church; it was able to function in a nonapocalyptic context. Thus church history shows the dispensable character of apoc-alypticism as "framework." What was not sufficiently realized was that the survival of the apocalyptic Christ depended on an ontologizing of the apocalyptic structures so that metaphysical speculation became the substitute of apocalyptic speculation in a nonapocalyptic world.

Once the Christian movement became a historical movement in the Roman Empire and had to accommodate itself within history and to historical structures, it underwent a "radical Hellenization." This meant an increasing ontologization of the gospel in terms of Greek speculative categories. The road toward this ontologization was historically mediated via apoc-alypticism and Gnosticism. Ultimately, the heavenly "furniture" of apocalyptic speculation became crucial building material for Christian metaphysical thought. In this process the latent specu-lative possibilities of the apocalyptic world view were made fruitful for the Logos-Christology of the church.[2] Thus apocalypticism could be shed as a "framework" only after its real contribution—the construction of a heavenly world with its divine personnel—was safeguarded and explored into a different direction by speculative thought.

A deapocalypticized Christ could only function as an ontologized Christ. Thus the fundamental significance of the apocalyptic world view for the construction of Christian dogma must be given its due place. Even where within the New Testament itself apocalyptic categories are deemphasized, the Jesus of history has been contaminated by an apocalyptic mind set, so that the Jesus of history has been displaced by an ontological-heavenly figure.

We seem driven to the conclusion that Paul not only uses apocalyptic language but also is imprisoned by the apocalyptic world view, so that his resurrection experience seems dictated by the apocalyptic world view and loses its validity without it. Experience and world view seem to be mutually dependent on each other, and it seems impossible with respect to Paul to construct a bridge to the New Testament resurrection experience.

B
The Religious Meaning of the Resurrection for Paul

In what sense, then, can the resurrection of Jesus Christ in Paul be interpreted as an expression of a new perception on reality, evoked by the historical Jesus? The profundity of the traditional "Jesus and Paul" problem lies exactly here. When we ask, *Of what* was the resurrection the experience for Paul?, we do not seem to receive an answer. If we say, The resurrection was the apocalyptic expression of *Paul's experience with Jesus,* we say more than the sources permit. Paul, as is well known, (1) does not seem to have known the historical Jesus and (2) is not interested in the life of Jesus.

The traditional search for incidental Synoptic Jesus sayings in the Pauline corpus cannot help here. For unless we can perceive the experience of Paul with Jesus behind the apocalyptic assertion of a risen Christ, we seem to have only two alternatives: either to assent to Paul's apocalyptic world view as properly ours or to reject it as unintelligible to us. But a third possible avenue to the solution of the "Jesus-Paul" problem may be suggested here. It involves a change of posture and perspective. Instead of focusing on the resurrection of Christ as proclaimed by Paul in an apocalyptic context, we look at the level of human conflict in Paul's life to which the resurrection of Jesus Christ becomes the religious and theological answer according to his own witness. In this way it may be possible to detect in terms of a hermeneutic of experience the function of resurrection language in Paul, namely, its function of resolving a conflict in his experience. This would constitute a concrete example of the negative and positive hermeneutical poles. The negative pole analyzes the components of the conflict in Paul's life, whereas the positive pole describes the restructuring of that conflict.

In what follows, I am using the term "resolution of conflict" advisedly. Although a hermeneutic of experience stresses a "restructuring of conflict" over against a "solution of conflict" because it does not believe in any final solutions within the range of present-day religious experience (cf. chapter 3), Paul seems to be making absolutistic claims for his "Christ"-experience. It often appears that the Christ-event for Paul is not just a restructuring of conflicts, but is claimed as a final tension-reducing solution. Thus, with respect to Paul, "resolution" terminology seems necessary in order to accent the ambiguity of Paul's use of resurrection language. Whether Paul with this "solution" terminology is faithful to Jesus' own intention remains open to question.

At any rate, along these lines, the apocalyptic world view with its resurrection language may be cracked open to reveal its religious functionality. It is in fact possible in terms of Paul's central theological dialectic to describe the basic conflict in his life.

That central dialectic revolves around the key concept of Paul's theology—"righteousness." There is good reason why Paul's thought revolves around *dikaiosvne* as the heart of the gospel (Romans 1:16), a concept which he never abandons even when translating his "Jewish" gospel to the "Greeks" (e.g., 1 Corinthians)—as Bultmann has adequately shown. *Dikaiosvne* is a real dialectical symbol, incorporating two basic conflictual aspects of Paul's experience. For when Paul comes to speak about *Israel's* tragedy in Romans 10:2 ("I bear them witness that they have a zeal for God, but it is not enlightened"), he seems to speak indirectly autobiographically—a point which can be substantiated by the specific autobiographical statements of Romans 7 which implements Romans 10:2 in important ways. The conflict in Paul's life to which "Jesus Christ" is the solution revolves, broadly speaking, around religious life as self-concern over against religious life as concern for others. To the central human question, What must I do to be saved? Paul found in the Judaism of his culture a profound answer: devotion to God in terms of commitment to God's self-revelation to Israel in his law. Zeal for God expresses itself in a pharisaic life-style of zeal for the law. This pharisaic life-style seemed to satisfy Paul's religious needs. The conflict—evoked and resolved by the story of Jesus—comes about because zeal for God under the law translates itself for Paul suddenly in ever greater introspective self-concern. Thus the law "given for life" (see Romans 7:10) is found to be death-dealing: my self-concern perverts my devotion to God. It deceives me in forcing me into a search for salvation-security, for elitism, for an "in-group" mentality. Thus Paul comes to see Israel's tragedy as his own. Its zeal for God is real, but misdirected. "It is not enlightened (Rom. 10:2)." It is out for itself: "For, being *ignorant* of the righteousness that comes from God, and seeking to establish their own, they did not submit to God's righteousness (Rom. 10:3)." The conflict then has a tragic element. It is not perceived as conflict, for it is blocked by "ignorance." The conflict in simple terms is structured by the dialectic of inevitable self-directedness and other-directedness; by the riddle that an illusion presides over life, namely, the illusion that the more intent I am on God, the more I am secretly out on securing life myself. Thus there is a demonic aspect to the law: it is given for "life," it commands me to obey its directions, but it never uncovers the deception in which I am caught, namely, the deception that ego concern is a prison which shuts life out. Thus the law stimulates my lust for life but does not change the futile direction of that lust.

At this point it is important to realize the post-hoc analysis of the conflict: Romans 7 and Romans 10 are therefore postconversion statements, as most interpreters realize. Two interpretative dangers must be avoided.

1. The first is a simple psychological description of Paul's life, an interpretation correctly rejected by authoritative twentieth-century neo-orthodox interpreters.[3] For such a psychological description is both illegitimate and impossible. It is impossible because the exegetical results indicate that Paul's Jewish life cannot be described as a life of despair under the burden of the law. In Christian perspective Paul indicts the Jew not for sticking to a law which the Jew consciously knows as a tyrant and deceiver and as incapable of fulfillment; rather, he indicts the Jew for his pride, his mistaken belief that life is obedience to a specified content of law which secretly reinforces self-concern. It is illegitimate because psychological descriptions are reductionistic and omit what is for Paul most central, i.e., the sudden incursion of the Christ-event in his life. In other words, they cannot explain why the Christ-event and not some other solution was embraced by Paul.

2. The opposite tendency has pointed out the reductionistic danger of a psychological description. Instead, it stresses the reality of the revelatory event, apart from any speculative incursions into Paul's psychological life. Thus it speaks about the *quando Deo visum est* (whenever it pleased God), about the divine initiative of the Christ-event which strikes an unprepared Paul as a bolt out of the blue and changes him. A hermeneutic of experience allows more sensitivity to both the continuous and discontinuous elements in Paul's conversion experience. It does not enter predictively into the conversion experience itself, as the psychological interpretation tends to do. Neither does it retreat into metaphysical resurrection and revelation language in order to safeguard the discontinuous element of the divine revelation. A hermeneutic of experience explores the conversion *ex eventu* (after the event); it investigates the interpretation Paul himself gives to his conversion and from there indicates the basic conflictual elements which Paul himself claims solved *after* the conversion experience. In other words, the conversion experience involves a shift of perception on Paul's part which he attributes to the Christ-event and which functions as revelatory and as decisive for the redirection of his life.

What we discern in Paul's life, then, is a particular linguistic interpretation of a sudden perceptual shift. The perceptual shift itself is hidden from us, but its functional outcome expresses itself in such a way that it allows us a look into the conflictual data to which the shift provided a solution; in other words, what is visible is the situation before the shift and after the shift. The shift itself is Paul's private experience and resists penetration; it is "Paul's revelatory moment." The *language* which expresses the perceptual shift is explicit *apocalyptic*-Christological language; Jesus Christ is the solution to Paul's original conflict. A delicate issue surfaces here. For Paul the Christ-event causes both the conflict and its resolution; a "natural" conflict—a natural dissatisfaction with Jewish life—was not solved by a "supernatural" answer. This reveals something about the revelatory-disclosure power of the moment of insight—the moment of the perceptual shift. It brings into conscious awareness what in Paul's case can only have been a latent or nascent possibility of conflict. Consequently, the kerygma in Paul's Christian life is not rational persuasion, not transmission of "Christian" information, however exalted, but it expresses the possibility of a perceptual shift which "Jesus Christ" occasions, a perceptual shift which involves both the bringing into awareness of conflictual elements and their resolution. Resolution language in Paul is explicit Christological language, i.e., it is apocalyptic language about a resurrected Christ. It is crucial to distinguish between two levels of Paul's use of language. The language is explicitly apocalyptic. It is the language of Paul's world view in terms of which he discusses the Christ-event. However, this theological-conceptual interpretative language is at times cracked open into its experiential components and can be expressed in other than explicit apocalyptic language. Thus the apocalyptic language can at times become hermeneutically "open" language, i.e., open to its actual function of bringing religious conflicts and resolutions to expression. Thus language functions at two levels in Paul: *explicit apocalyptic language* and *symbolic "apocalyptic" language.*

The real question, however, is: To what extent was the apocalyptic conceptuality an appropriate tool to bring Paul's experience to expression? When Paul brings his experience into language, is the given language of the culture an appropriate language, i.e., is it "therapeutic" or "pathological" language? At this point we can only be certain about the hermeneutical issue; *for us* the apocalyptic language with its reifying tendencies operates as "closure" language, or as pathological language. Whether this was true historically as well for Paul is another matter. We cannot uncover the strength or weakness of apocalypticism for Paul's own experience. Paul may not have had any other option in any case. Yet it would seem quite possible that apocalypticism is intrinsically "bad" language and that an apocalyptic interpretation of Christ was a historical perversion of Jesus' message.

The only criterion we have for evaluating Paul's experience, then, is not his language about it but its function in his life. And on this point we can be sure: Paul does not just make verbal claims about Christ, he does not just change his vocabulary, but a fundamental new commitment and direction in his life has come about through the "Christ-event."

"Apocalyptic"-symbolic language: The function of Christ language is apparent in Paul's description of the fruit of the Christ-event: it means to him essentially a new direction to his life, one which seems to epitomize the description of outwardness and openness in chapter 2. Thus the meaning of the Christ experience for Paul is mission; Paul now becomes *the* apostle to the Gentiles (Galatians 1:16) and preaches Christ crucified as the sole life-giving power for mankind. The new direction in Paul's life is bound up with the cross of Christ as the dynamic behind Paul's interpretation of "life in Christ." Thus "Christ crucified and risen" is in Paul a dialectical symbol which may enable us to unpack Paul's existential conflicts and their resolution. Christ crucified and risen means for Paul that life under the law is cracked open and that life is now experienced as a gift—a gift which man receives as the by-product of a completely new direction in his life, namely, the direction of spending one's life not in search for self but for others. If this analysis is at all correct, it suggests that the Christ-event in Paul is not simply an apocalyptic heavenly incursion, an isolated mind-blowing miracle, with no recourse to the life of Jesus. Rather the Christ-event in Paul is open to the story of Jesus—crucified and

risen—which Paul received from the early Christian community, which antagonized him, which he sought to destroy—but which finally convicted him. The function of Christological language in Paul, then, suggests that Paul stumbled over the story of a Jewish Messiah who spent his life for others and was crucified and yet vindicated by God. The conflictual components behind the perceptual shift seem to constitute one of man's permanent problems: lust for life and losing one's life for others to gain it.

Thus "Christ language" and "resurrection language" function as an amazing parallel to Jesus' understanding of life before God: "Whoever seeks to gain his life will lose it, but whoever loses his life will preserve it" (Luke 17:33; cf. Matt. 10:39; 16:25; Mark 8:35; Luke 9:24; John 12:25).

"Apocalyptic"-explicit language: Why, however, is it so difficult to trace Paul's relation to the story of Jesus and its evocative character for his life?

The difficulty is obviously the apocalyptic world view, so alien to us and so much the natural house of language for Paul. There is a double difficulty on this point. We must ask not only the question of our alienation from Paul's world view but also the more important question: Is Paul's world view and its language appropriate to the experience he intends to describe? Or even more radically: Was Paul's apocalyptic world view with its resurrection language appropriate to Jesus' fundamental intention?

At this point I would suggest that the apocalyptic world view is singularly inappropriate to explicate Paul's religious experience, if this experience was indeed triggered by the story of Jesus. For the apocalyptic world view tends to reify and ontologize the experiential components of the perceptual shift. Thus apocalyptic language tends to be closure language—it veers away from the religious experience; it tends to ossify and rigidify language which must be open to experience. Thus apocalyptic language ceases to be symbolic language and tends to become abstract-conceptual language. Apocalyptic language resists unpacking because of its abstract-metaphysical tendencies. Thus "Jesus Christ" and "the risen Christ" as used by Paul seem to function *for us* as rigid concepts—not as linguistic interpretations of religious experience but as divine data and as divine realities without apparent empirical grounding in the life of Jesus. Reified language, then, ceases to be symbolic language but becomes metaphysical reality.

The functional danger of such apocalyptic language in Paul is that "Jesus Christ" becomes a rigid theological concept which answers all existential questions in advance. Too often in Paul, not the God of the death-of-God theologians but Jesus Christ becomes the problem solver. Thus the intrinsic criticism to be raised against Paul is: To what extent is the religious language of Jesus, evoking men to commitment action, transformed into a theological concept, "Jesus Christ," which now operates as a universal solution device? And the critical question about Paul's theology remains: To what extent has speculative apocalyptic language displaced symbolic religious language as the expression of an experienced Jesus?

For a man not conditioned by the apocalyptic world view and not living within its boundaries, it seems that the apocalyptic drama of an imminent Parousia, the resurrection as part of that drama, and a populated heavenly world fall away. It almost seems that for Paul the figure of Jesus drowns out before the drama of a cult hero's death and resurrection, so that Christ does not function as the apostle's living experience of Jesus but as an existential symbol of dying and rising—similar to one of the mystery-religions of Paul's day—as conditions for a true human life.

The resurrection of Jesus, then, is for a hermeneutic of experience not an isolated apocalyptic event, a heavenly incursion into earthly circumstance, but the articulation within a particular world view (apocalypticism) of a basic experience which Jesus evoked and continues to evoke. Any interpretations of Paul must face the risk that Paul may have misunderstood Jesus' intention and that his apocalyptic-rabbinic world view may have reinstated what Jesus wanted to deemphasize. The possibility remains that Paul's experience of Jesus has been contaminated by the theological "bag" which Paul brought to his Christian experience. In this sense the church wisely prefaced the Pauline corpus with the four-fold Gospel and has resisted since the time of Marcion the speculative-Gnostic implications of Pauline theology. Thus a hermeneutic of experience is vitally interested in the Gospels as portrayals of experience evoked by the historical Jesus. A hermeneutic of experience views Jesus as the catalytic agent of a new perception on reality which is experienced as grace and rebirth—as total surprise, as revelatory.

The weight of an experiential interpretation of the resurrection, then, does not rest on the language or the objectivity of the event, guaranteed by the language, but on the new articulation given to the experience of Jesus, namely, that he is the Christ, that in him a new experience is opened up which can only be articulated as God's activity in and through Jesus. The crux of the matter thus is not the materialistic and descriptive content of the resurrection experience—as if its validity is enhanced by stressing the materialistic and objective features of a risen Christ—but the person who generates it and its new impact on the life of the experiencer.

A hermeneutic of experience does not emphasize the transmission of information about Jesus or about his resurrection so that my salvation depends on assent to apostolic propositions about Jesus' resurrection. Rather a hermeneutic of experience concentrates on the re-creation of a particular type of experience and its ultimate source in Jesus. Thus a hermeneutic of experience suggests its own future lines of research. Indeed, everything remains tentative until the relation of Jesus to the Synoptic Gospels is clarified. For unless it can be demonstrated in what specific ways Jesus moved within the apocalyptic climate of his time—how much he affirmed and how much he rejected and/or corrected—the appeal to the historical Jesus as the catalytic agent of a specific type of religious experience is an ideological construct, as suspect in its own right as the modernized versions of the life of Jesus so correctly rejected by Albert Schweitzer. If the evidence warrants it, a hermeneutic of experience would favor the recent "Jewish" interpretation of Jesus as climaxing the line of Old Testament prophets. In this way the debunking attitude of classical Old Testament prophecy described in chapter 5 would find its hermeneutical focus in the very heart of New Testament religion.

Why is Jesus crucial as the source of this religious experience? Simply because Christianity claims to be a way of life and not an idealistic philosophy. For a hermeneutic of experience God's act in Jesus Christ entails two fundamental assertions: the experience is evoked by a person who (1) proclaims a way of life *as one of us,* as subject to our conditions, and (2) is yet able *to act out* this way of life amid the ambiguities of history. Otherwise the experience may be a pseudo-experience, an idealistic construct—ascribed to Jesus, but actually a theory or language event which has never been "enfleshed" and is incapable of such enfleshment. Thus every Christian assertion must ultimately be validated by the Jesus of history—not so much to reconstruct a "Jesus as he really was" but to guarantee its earthiness and concreteness.

The historical Jesus guarantees not only the historical, this-worldly, public *source* of our experience but also its this-worldly *intention,* so that the experience becomes inseparable from commitment to ethical action in this world. In this sense our hermeneutical reflections tend to lend support to radical outwardness and openness as the two fundamental poles of people's experience with Jesus.

part four

The
Theological
Future

commitment without ideology

Our argument has been admittedly speculative throughout, although not without considerable support. We have attempted to push its implications as far as possible in an attempt to suggest next steps for exploration. Often this has led into areas where existing data are sketchy or even nonexistent. Or a new cast has been put on old questions so that what had seemed self-evident must be examined again. In this concluding statement we will not attempt to raise any further questions, only pull together the major themes of the argument in a summary fashion.

The dominant theme has been that the Christian is called to commitment but not to any ideology. He is not called to be committed to the idea of a triune God, a risen Christ, or even the man Jesus. Rather, his commitment is to a *growth process* in the direction of *responsible action* expressed in increased concern for others and openness to future change. As the authority for his action he cannot appeal to a divine decree expressed in the law of God or to an apocalyptic view of the risen Christ living within him; he cannot appeal to any ideology which gives him a corner on determining what is right and good and true. Generalizing from chapter 5, the authority of the man of faith is limited to (1) the conviction of vision which his own growth has produced but in the very production has also relativized, (2) his increasingly universal scope of concern through which he experiences the needs of an increasing number of others as his own, and (3) norms for action intrinsic to a given situation. These intrinsic norms cannot be abstracted into general principles, for they are situation specific. Further, they are always subject to review, for they lack the backing of any ideology. Given his changed need perception, the Christian acts in response to the needs of others just as he acts to meet his own needs. The action taken emerges out of the contingencies of the need situation as he perceives it, not from some divine mandate. It is flexible. When the situation and/or his perception changes, his course of action may change.

This growth process in the direction of responsible and flexible action, while ongoing, is characterized by radical perceptual shifts. The change involved is not simply maturational or the result of an increase in resolve and effort. It is a change in the perceptual structures undergirding one's very reality; the way one sees himself and his world. No longer is his focus strictly inward. His gaze is thrust outward; others are seen as neighbor. Such a perceptual shift, characteristic of creative growth, is the result of the breakdown of one's existing reality. Cracks form so that it no longer functions; one is brought to a standstill. For example, as discussed in chapter 6, with Paul this occurred in a dramatic way when he became aware of the basically self-centered character of adherence to the law. Seeking to move beyond self-concern, he found he was becoming even more self-obsessed.

In evaluating whether a given experience such as Paul's is creative (i.e., involves growth) the basic criterion is *how it functions:* Does it extend the range of the person's reality rather than constricting it? Many religious experiences do not involve growth. They are flights away from the nakedness of facing one's own relativity and vulnerability, flight into the secure womb of dependence on something outside oneself which provides meaning and direction in all circumstances. "Christ is the answer." "Jesus is the Way." An ideology is born. Meaning and direction are found, but at what cost? The tragedy of such ideological answers is that blinders are an essential part of the purchase. One is forced to see himself and his world as the answer dictates. The result is often ostensibly that in the name of love and concern for others one is unable to perceive and respond to their experienced needs. The answer dictates a priori what their needs are. They need an all-inclusive answer. And if we can convince them of this, we have made ourselves a little more secure in our conviction that our answer is indeed *the* unshakable truth. In contrast, Christian growth involves a weaning from a need for *the* truth and a movement toward an open and flexible concern for others.

What makes this growth Christian? It seems to be the kind of growth Jesus sought to evoke. As we have seen, however, the attempt to determine with confidence the kind of growth for which Jesus served as a catalyst is fraught with difficulty. Between us and any direct encounter with Jesus lies an immense culture gap. This gap is further widened by the mediation of the experience of the early church in response to him and its linguistic expression of this experience in the biblical record, an expression necessarily framed in the concep-tuality of their apocalyptic rabbinic or Gnostic world views. Paul's letters, though temporally closest to Jesus, are heavily laden with apocalypticism, making it extremely difficult to recapture the experiential base of which they are the expres-sion. And, as noted in the last chapter, apocalypticism placed a heavy hand even upon the Synoptic Gospels, especially in the birth and resurrection stories. The historical Jesus seems hidden from us behind an apocalyptic mask.

In contrast, apocalyptic influence is relatively absent in the Old Testament. In its rich literature there are a number of linguistic forms which seem directed toward generation of a religious perceptual shift in the hearer. And, as suggested in chapter 5, much of this language seems to be directed toward a common purpose: The metaphysical mythologies of the ancient Near East, both outside and within Israel, are continually de-bunked. Ideologies are brought low, and the hearer is continu-ally challenged to take responsibility for his action rather than simply casting it as a bit part in a cosmological drama under divine direction. As a result of their cultural marginality, the Israelites are able to see the relativity of the competing ideologies of the day. Myth is replaced by history and narrative as forms of linguistic expression. Man begins to take responsibility for writing his own script.

By the time of the New Testament, however, eschatology has given way to apocalyptic. History itself has become a stage on which a grand drama of personal salvation is enacted. Man is replaced by superman, the first Adam by the last. Jesus is the Christ who through God's Act has conquered death, the prototype of what man can and should be. Man surrenders his responsibility to a conceptuality which is often just as ideological and oppressive as the mythologies the Israelites debunked.

Is this what Jesus intended? Obviously, the question is extremely difficult and will probably never yield to a satisfactory answer. But in the context of Part Three it can be sharpened a bit to suggest its implications. On the one hand, to what degree was Jesus' call to "repent, for the kingdom of God is at hand" simply an expression of the apocalyptic *Geist* of his day? Or, on the other hand, was it an attempt to debunk apocalypticism, challenging one to see the kingdom not as "beyond" but on earth in the lives of men? If his intent was the former, there is truly a radical break between the Old and New Testaments, a break just as sharp as between Israelite debunking and Greek idealism as styles of thought. Consciously or not, Jesus then becomes an opportunist shrewdly capitalizing on the wave of the future, playing an apocalyptic role for an increasingly apocalyptic age. If, however, his intent was the latter, he stands squarely in the line of the Old Testament prophets, debunking the new personal salvation ideology of apocalypticism and challenging his hearers to shift their focus of concern from personal salvation to the neighbor. Then Jesus is not seen as claiming to have fulfilled the apocalypticized hope for a Messiah or Christ. Rather, he invokes the language of apocalyptic precisely to deapocalypticize it, to free it from metaphysical reification and to ground it in lived experience. Terms such as "Son of God" and "Son of man" come to function as symbolic expressions of the significance of his challenge for the lives of men in this world. But then it is also true that to the extent that some New Testament writings reapocalypticize Jesus, they would seem to involve a serious distortion of his intent.

Clearly, either interpretation has its evidence pro and con and its costs as well as its benefits. But on the basis of our examination of the writing and cultural context of both the Old and New Testaments, especially the linguistic form of Jesus' sayings and parables as presented in the Synoptics, we tend to favor the latter alternative. Jesus seems more Hebrew than Christian, as this latter term has come to be understood. Therefore, we have attempted to suggest a reconception of what it means to be Christian, not ignoring the use of the term over the past two thousand years but trying to get behind the ideological overlay to the growth experience which seems closer to Jesus' debunking concern.

In so doing we have proposed a new hermeneutical method based on an examination of the psychodynamics of religious growth experiences, a hermeneutic of experience. This method attempts to probe the symbolic religious language of the Bible, seeking to unpack the elements of the perceptual shift experience it contains. First, one seeks to uncover the existential conflict which promoted the experience the writer is seeking to express. Then the restructuring of the conflict can be examined for its functional efficacy in the writer's own cultural and social world. The intent is not to discover answers which we can adopt but to suggest clues for ways of seeing our world differently so that we may live more responsibly.

Our attempt has been to sketch a new way for doing theology. We hope that it is not a dead-end street, and that critical response may aid us on our way. Many uncertainties remain. Chief among them will be the question of whether our definition of ideology is sufficiently sharp as not to be open to the charge of a new ideology, i.e., a tacit assumption about the necessity of human growth and the Gospel's appeal to it. Why appeal to the Gospel when, both in the New Testament and in church history, proclamation is so differently understood from its discussion in this book? Why appeal to Jesus when he is both so historically hidden from us and seemingly so apocalyptically determined? Do we simply present a Harnack Jesus under a Merleau-Ponty robe? And on a philosophical level, have we not scarcely scratched the surface on the difficult question of the relation between language and experience? None of these questions has been satisfactorily answered, but we hope that the questions have at least been sharpened and will point the way to future inquiry.

notes

introduction

1. Ideology, since the term was coined by Destutt de Tracy at the end of the eighteenth century and radicalized by Marx (Karl Marx and Frederick Engels, *The German Ideology* [New York: International Publishers, 1947]), has most frequently been used to speak of political ideologies. Therefore, it should be pointed out that we are using the term here in a more general sense. Any systematic world view or description of reality is an ideology, whether political, religious, scientific, or whatever. In this general application we are using ideology in Karl Mannheim's "total" sense of "not merely the content but also the form, and even the conceptual framework of a mode of thought" *(Ideology and Utopia* [New York: Harcourt, Brace & World, 1936], p. 57). And with Mannheim we would agree that an ideology always belongs to a "concrete historico-social group"; it defines a social context as well as a reality. Largely due to Mannheim, this more general conception of ideology has become dominant in the sociology of knowledge. It is not accidental that ideology first emerged as a prominent analytic concept in the sociology of knowledge, for without the comparative analysis of realities for different social groups, any distinction between reality as ontologically valid and ideology as one's interpretation of experience is forever masked.

For an excellent discussion of the history of the term "ideology," see *Ideology and Utopia,* chap. 2. More recently, political ideologies have received considerable attention in the "end of ideology" discussion (cf. Daniel Bell, *The End of Ideology* [Glencoe, Ill.: Free Press, 1960], and Chaim I. Waxman, ed., *The End of Ideology Debate* [New York: Funk & Wagnalls, 1968]).

2. A word must be said about "metaphysical" and "ontological" as we are using these terms, for they will appear frequently. Throughout the history of Western philosophy metaphysical has generally meant a systematic description of true reality which transcends human experience. In general, ontology involves an analysis of being-in-itself or essence. These terms are used in this manner by idealist, existentialist, realist, and process metaphysicians (though, of course, the content of their respective metaphysics and ontologies differ radically) and by positivists in their critiques of metaphysics. Since these philosophies are the dominant ones undergirding recent theology, these general definitions will be used here as well.

More recently, however, existential phenomenology has sought to redefine metaphysics and ontology. Maurice Merleau-Ponty speaks of metaphysics as transcending the linguistic and conceptual reality of our everyday world not by a move upward toward an absolute reality but by a recovery of the roots of our constructed reality in prelinguistic and prereflective experience. Being and ontology are similarly reconceived, neither as involving the essential ground of experience or the distilled absolute facts of experience but to speak of the fabric of lived experience itself, "wild Being." "The 'answer' is higher than the 'facts,' lower than the 'essences,' in the wild Being where they were, and—behind or beneath the cleavages of our acquired culture—continue to be, undivided" *(The Visible and the Invisible,* trans. Alphonso Lingis [Evanston, Ill.: Northwestern University Press, I968], p. 121). Although this transcending-into-experience conception of metaphysics and ontology is quite compatible with the experiential theology proposed here, it is clearly juxtaposed to the more customary use of these terms. In an attempt to be as clear as possible we shall only use metaphysical and ontological as they have been more traditionally used. Accordingly, existential phenomenology is neither metaphysical nor ontological as those terms will be used here. Yet it is not actively opposed to traditional metaphysics and ontology as is positivism, for to be actively opposed assumes acceptance of the traditional definitions. Rather, it finds such concerns unfruitful and misleading in its attempt to examine the experienced basis of our everyday world. Traditional metaphysical and ontological questions simply are not asked. Therefore, existential phenomenology may be best characterized as a-metaphysical and a-ontological.

chapter 1   the function of the bible today
1. Much of what follows appeared in an earlier version in an article, "Reflections on Biblical Theology," *Interpretation,* July 1970, pp. 303-20.

chapter 2   growth in response to jesus
1. Harvey Cox, *The Feast of Fools: A Theological Essay on Festivity and Fantasy* (Cambridge, Mass.: Harvard University Press, 1969), p. 165. Used by permission.
2. Although the functional character of religious and specifically Christian experience is discussed in some detail in chapter 3, initial definitions seem necessary here. Rather than defining an experience as religious on the basis of its content or referent (e.g., an experience *of* God, oneness, ultimacy, or personal transcendence) we shall consider an experience to be religious if it is generated by "religious existential conflicts." These are conflicts which challenge one's reality at its core, e.g., "What is the meaning of life, given death?" or "How shall I live with my fellowman?" Any experience in which one attempts to deal with such conflicts we shall call religious. Given such a definition, Christian experience is a subgroup within religious experience (since there are non-Christian ways to deal with such conflicts) in which the experience assumes a Christian direction, moving the person toward increasingly responsible involvement with a growing social environment. If Jesus is the impetus for such growth, the experience is explicitly Christian; if not, it is only implicitly so. This last distinction is made for clarity only and will not be used subsequently. Obviously, there is an immense danger of profaning another's perception of his experience to call it implicitly Christian. Perhaps it is best simply to rejoice when growth in such a direction occurs, not imposing one's own external categories upon it at all.
3. Cf. Jesus' parables of the talents and of those heirs of the kingdom who served him in their fellowman (Matthew 25:14-46) as well as the epistle of James for clear insistence upon the necessity of this connection.

4. As I shall attempt to make clear below, in the link of perceptions and prereflective conception I am following the French existential phenomenologist Maurice Merleau-Ponty (see especially, *The Visible and the Invisible* [Evanston, III.: Northwestern University Press, 1968]) and human-information-processing theorists in psychology such as H.M. Schroder, O.J. Harvey, and J.McV. Hunt.

5. It should, of course, be noted that Jesus not only challenges those who claim to be at least attempting to live up to the demands of the Jewish law, the scribes and pharisees, but he also challenges the "publicans and sinners" (see e.g., the call of Zacchaeus, Luke 19:1-9).

6. For a discussion of Jesus' use of *abba,* see Joachim Jeremias, *The Central Message of the New Testament* (New York: Charles Scribner's Sons, 1965), chap. 1.

7. The function of the community as a support base for one's individual ministry is but one pole of a dialectic, the other being the potential power which any community has within a society as an institution. With the potential for institutional power, however, comes a tendency toward institutional calcification and lethargy, for institutional power lies in clearly defined and broadly based structures. The dialectic exists, for it seems clear that Christianity as a communal faith cannot exist in any form other than institutional structure, but it seems equally clear that the Christian message provides a continuing critical challenge to any existing structure. This challenge seems to take form not only in reformation within the church but also in a continual movement of the church outside itself (i.e., outside its institutional structures) to more fluid (but thereby politically less powerful) forms.

8. Jesus' challenge to the "rich young man" (Mark 10:17ff.) seems to illustrate this process. In the course of their exchange Jesus enables this young man to recognize that it has not been his answer to the question "What must I do to inherit eternal life?" which is in error, but the question itself. The "answer" Jesus gives forces a change of focus away from this question to "How may I serve my fellowman?," a question the young man is not ready to face.

9. In a similar manner Dietrich Bonhoeffer notes in "Thoughts on the Baptism of D.W.R.," "We have spent too much time thinking, supposing that if only we weigh every possibility in advance, everything will somehow happen automatically. We have learnt a bit too late in the day that action springs not from thought, but from readiness for responsibility. For you thought and action will have a new relationship. Your thinking will be confined to your responsibilities in action. With us thought was often the luxury of the looker-on; with you it will be entirely subordinated to action." *(Letters and Papers from Prison* [New York: Macmillan, 1967], p. 184.)

10. John MacQuarrie places a somewhat similar emphasis upon the centrality of openness for the Christian message in *God-talk* (New York: Harper & Row, 1967), pp. 208ff. Especially suggestive is his contention that the way we use openness today seems very close to the use of the symbol of "light" for the biblical writers. For the man of that day light was the requisite for action. Light rendered possible as well as revealing the need for action.

11. By "post-neo-orthodox theologians" I refer to those who have grown up professionally in a neo-orthodox context but have clearly moved beyond it. Many seem to remain post-neo-orthodox, however, because although they have today moved beyond neo-orthodoxy in the content and style of their theologizing, few seem to have been able to extricate themselves from the latent philosophical assumptions undergirding neo-orthodoxy. Although the answers which they provide are quite new and refreshing, the questions are strangely familiar: How

can we speak of God meaningfully today? What is the meaning of incarnation for modern secular man? How can we recapture the experience of the transcendent realm? What is God's plan for history? What is God's Word for man? What is the Christian concept of man? Such questions seem to be founded on an idealist or realist philosophy, for they seek the nature of reality. A process metaphysic, though providing different answers, focuses upon much the same sort of questions. In contrast, the present attempt to work from assumptions grounded in existential phenomenology places such questions themselves under question, asking whether a particular conception of reality is not actually antithetical to Christian experience.

12. For an analysis of the metaphysic within Barth's theology, see John B. Cobb, Jr., *Living Options in Protestant Theology: A Survey of Methods* (Philadelphia: Westminster Press, 1962), chap. 7.

13. It should be noted that the shift of emphasis needed is not from attention to one type of metaphysical conception to another, from an otherworldly cosmology to a metaphysic of the person or Self, to a process metaphysic, or to a metaphysic of history and the future. The proposed shift is rather from any attempt to describe reality to a focus on the commitment-action experience of Christian growth.

14. For a similar characterization of the nature of religious language, see Ian T. Ramsey's analysis of "commitment-discernment" language in *Religious Language* (New York: Macmillan, 1957).

15. For further elaboration of this *extremely* brief sketch of Merleau-Ponty's existential phenomenology, see his major works: *The Structure of Behavior,* trans. A.L. Fisher (Boston: Beacon Press, 1963); *Phenomenology of Perception,* trans. Colin Smith (New York: Humanities Press, 1962); *Sense and Non-Sense,* trans. H.L. and P.A. Dreyfus (Evanston, Ill.: Northwestern University Press, 1964); and *The Primacy of Perception,* ed. James M. Edie (Evanston, Ill.: Northwestern University Press, 1964); as well as the previously cited *The Visible and the Invisible.*

16. Merleau-Ponty presents a nice example of this affirmation-negation process in speaking of the primordial in *The Visible and the Invisible:*

"We say therefore that our body is a being of two leaves, from one side a thing among things and otherwise what sees them and touches them; we say, because it is evident, that it unites these two properties within itself, and its double belongingness to the order of the "object" and to the order of the "subject" reveals to us quite unexpected relations between the two orders. . . . *One should not even say, as we did a moment ago, that the body is made up of two leaves,* of which the one, that of the 'sensible,' is bound up with the rest of the world. There are not in it two leaves or layers; fundamentally it is neither thing seen only nor seer only, it is visibility sometimes wandering and sometimes reassembled." (P. 137, italics added.)

17. This use of "odd" is borrowed from Ramsey, *Religious Language.*

18. Langdon Gilkey, *Naming the Whirlwind: The Renewal of God-Language* (Indianapolis, Ind.: Bobbs-Merrill, 1969), p.468.

19. I suspect an exegetical rendering of this for modern man as "What business is that of yours?" or "Don't sweat it" is far more tenable than the attempts to make this statement a revelation by God of his nature. This passage and the a-metaphysical character of Israelite language generally is discussed in detail in chapters 4 and 5.

20. For the basic discussion of "falsification," see Antony Flew and Alasdair MacIntyre, eds., *New Essays in Philosophical Theology* (New York: Macmillan, 1955), chap.6, "Theology and Falsification."

21. H. Richard Niebuhr's "confessional theology" maintains a thrust quite similar to that proposed here.

22. The Christian cannot, however, simply reify the mystery, awe, or wonder (as seems to occur in much Eastern mysticism), for the thrust of the call of Jesus is always toward the social world seen anew, not away from it.

23. At this point a basic difference between the position suggested here and Rudolf Bultmann's emphasis upon the *kerygma* emerges. The kerygmatic emphasis tends to conceptualize Jesus and his message, rather than simply allowing him to speak. Bultmann's assertion that Christianity must make an existential difference for the believer seems sound, but the interaction he develops is largely between a conceptual message and man rather than between the person who confronts him through the biblical record and man. Of course, Bultmann is no neo-fundamentalist, asking assent to a conceptual package; he is far too aware for that. But for him the catalyst for the life of faith lies in the Christian message itself. The experiential level of the life lived in response to Jesus' challenging in love, the source of the message, seems lost.

chapter 3   the re-creative power of the word of god

1. Max Wertheimer, *Productive Thinking* (New York: Harper & Brothers, 1945), pp. 235-36.

2. See, for example, Freud's *Leonardo da Vinci: A Study in Psychosexuality* (New York: Random House, 1916). For an annotated bibliography of the extensive literature on the relation of Freud's concept of sublimation to creative thought, see Morris I. Stein and Shirley J. Heinze, *Creativity and the Individual* (Glencoe, Ill.: Free Press, 1960), pp. 203-24.

3. "On Preconscious Mental Processes," *Psychoanalytic Quarterly* 19 (1950): 540-60, reprinted in David Rapaport, *Organization and Pathology of Thought: Selected Sources* (New York: Columbia University Press, 1951) and quoted from there, pp. 487-88. A similar view is also expressed by Rapaport himself in his concluding essay in that volume, pp. 720-21, and by R. Shafer in "Regression in the Service of the Ego," in Gardner Lindzey, ed., *Assessment of Human Motives* (New York: Rinehart, 1958), pp. 119-48. For similar views but which do not use the phrase "regression in the service of the ego," see Eliot D. Hutchinson, *How to Think Creatively* (New York: Abingdon, 1959), especially pp. 38-41 and 146-47; V.H. Rosen, "Some Aspects of the Role of Imagination in Psychoanalysis," *Journal of the American Psychoanalytic Association,* 8 (1960): 229-51; J. Nydes, "Creativity and Psychotherapy," *Psychoanalytic Review,* 49:1 (1962): 29-33; and D. Beres, "Perception, Imagination and Reality," *International Journal of Psychoanalysis,* 41 (1960): 327-34.

4. See Lawrence Kubie, *Neurotic Distortion of the Creative Process* (Lawrence, Kans.: University of Kansas Press, 1958), especially pp. 39-52. See also the Kubie-oriented research of Holland and Baird reported in "The Pre-conscious Activity Scale: The Development and Validation of an Originality Measure," *Journal of Creative Behavior* 2:3 (1968): 217-25.

5. This emphasis is evident in the contributions of Fromm, May, Rogers, and Maslow to H.M. Anderson, ed., *Creativity and Its Cultivation* (New York: Harper & Brothers, 1959), in Horney's *Neurosis and Human Growth* (New York: W.W. Norton & Co., 1951), and in Maslow's *Toward a Psychology of Being* (Princeton, N.J.: D. Van Nostrand Co., 1962). Gilbert Rose presents a somewhat similar view with his "ego expansion" model in "Creative Imagination in Terms of Ego 'Core' and Boundaries," *International Journal of Psychoanalysis* 45:1 (1964): 75-84.

6. Graham Wallas, *The Art of Thought* (New York: Harcourt Brace, 1926).

7. Harold Rugg, *Imagination* (New York: Harper & Row, 1963), p. 289.

8. For a general introduction to the information-processing approach to psychology, cf. O.J. Harvey, D.E. Hunt, and Harold M. Schroder, *Conceptual Systems and Personality Organization* (New York: John Wiley & Sons, 1961), Schroder, M.J. Driver, and S. Streufert, *Human Information Processing* (New York: Holt, Rinehart and Winston, 1967), and Schroder and Peter Suedfeld, eds., *Personality Theory and Information Processing* (New York: Ronald Press, 1971). The information-processing theorist who has given the most attention to creativity is Marvin Karlins. In addition to his doctoral dissertation, "Conceptual Complexity and Remote Associative Proficiency as Creativity Variables in a Complex Problem Solving Task" (1966), see "Some Empirical Evidence for an Exploration Stage in the Creative Process," *Journal of Creative Behavior* 2:4 (1968): 256-62, and Karlins and Schroder, "Discovery, Learning, Creativity, and the Inductive Teaching Program," *Psychological Reports* 20 (1967): 867-76. I have developed the link between an information-processing model of creativity and religious experience in "Creativity and Religious Development: Toward a Structural-Functional Psychology of Religion" (unpublished Th.D. dissertation, Princeton Theological Seminary, 1971).

9. A strikingly similar demythologization of "unconscious" in terms of the structures of reality is presented by Merleau-Ponty; see *The Structure of Behavior* (Boston: Beacon Press, 1963) and *The Visible and the Invisible* (Evanston, Ill.: Northwestern University Press, 1968). The coincidence is not totally surprising, for the information-processing theorists owe some philosophical debts to phenomenology and both owe psychological debts to Gestalt theory.

10. There are, of course, many problems which are creatively "solved," i.e., problems or conflicts which require a shift in only one aspect of one's reality to account for the experience in question (e.g., Einstein's theory of relativity). Mathematical problems, because they occur within a self-consciously constructed reality, are often of this type. As will become clear in discussing creative Christian growth, we are talking here about a more pervasive sort of conflict, one which challenges the core of one's reality in a profound way, and to speak of resolution of these conflicts seems to oversimplify the situation considerably. Creativity at the level considered here does not contradict the more circumspect analysis of creative solutions; it is simply a different process.

11. In addition to its basis in information-processing theory, this summary owes considerable debt to James Loder's "hypnagogic paradigm" outlined in *Religious Pathology and Christian Faith* (Philadelphia: Westminster Press, 1966). Charles Hampden-Turner also presents a rather similar model of the creative process in *Radical Man* (Cambridge, Mass.: Schenkman, 1970).

12. James, *Varieties of Religious Experience* (New York: Longmans, Green and Co., 1902), p. 275, quoting from H.D. Thoreau, *Walden,* Riverside edition, p. 206, abridged.

13. James, *Varieties,* p. 250, quoting from E.D. Starbuck, *The Psychology of Religion* (London: Walter Scott, 1899).

14. James, *Varieties,* pp. 212-14, quoting from Edward's and Dwight's *Life of Brainerd* (New Haven: 1822), pp. 45-47, abridged.

15. From *The Varieties of Psychedelic Experience* by R.E.L. Masters and Jean Houston, p. 292. Copyright © 1966 by R.E.L. Masters and Jean Houston. Reprinted by permission of Holt, Rinehart and Winston, Inc.

16. Ibid., pp. 295-96.

17. Ibid., p. 298.

18. Since both the structural and functional characteristics of potentially creative

symbolic language are developed elsewhere (C. Daniel Batson, "How Far Does One Teach the Truth Which Admits of Being Learned?: Toward a Model of Education for Creative Growth," *Religious Education* 66:3 [1971]:180-91), the presentation here will attempt no defense of the characterization of potentially creative symbolic language, only a summary of it.

19. It should be noted that this initial statement of the semantic dialectic involves no hypothesis of a one-to-one correlation between language and an "objective reality." The possibility of a "true" or "perfect" language such as that sought by the logical atomists, notably Bertrand Russell and the early Ludwig Wittgenstein (see his *Tractatus Logico-Philosophicus,* trans. O.F. Pears and B.F. McGuiness [London: Routledge and Kegan Paul, 1926]) is not espoused. The dialectical process noted involves not a "matching" of word and thing but a restructuring of the phenomena at a linguistic level (see Wittgenstein's later *Philosophical Investigations,* trans. G.E.M. Anscombe [New York: Macmillan, 1953]). As Peter Berger and Thomas Luckmann suggest in *The Social Construction of Reality* (Garden City, N.Y.: Doubleday, 1966), it is only at the level of language that "reality" actually emerges, for it is a social construction.

20. Originally by William Chapman during his graduate study at Princeton Theological Seminary, 1967.

21. Susanne Langer, *Philosophy in a New Key* (New York: New American Library, 1942), pp. 152-53.

22. The term dialectical symbol, and its structural-functional nature, was developed by J. Randall Nichols and myself while working on a joint project in the spring of 1967. Therefore, in the discussion of it, I am considerably in his debt.

23. Chapter 4 extends the discussion of this symbolic kernelizing process considerably, noting specific examples of its use in the Old Testament.

24. Others who have emphasized the experiential base of language as key are Berger and Luckmann, *The Social Construction of Reality;* Langer, *Philosophy in a New Key;* John MacQuarrie, *God-talk* (New York: Harper & Row, 1967); and Ian T. Ramsey, *Religious Language* (New York: Macmillan, 1957).

25. Ramsey, *Religious Language,* p. 61; see also pp. 90-91.

26. It should be noted, however, that recent psychological research on intrinsic motivation suggests that it is quite possible either to encourage or inhibit the willingness and ability of an individual to encounter such a conflict over a longer period in the individual's developmental history. See O.J. Harvey, ed., *Motivation and Social Interaction* (New York: Ronald Press, 1963), especially chap. 3 by J.McV. Hunt, "Motivation Inherent in Information Processing and Action," pp. 35-94. Also, for intriguing educational examples of encouraging motivation to encounter conflict, see A.S. Neill, *Summerhill* (New York: Hart, 1960), and George B. Leonard, *Education and Ecstasy* (New York: Delacorte Press, 1968).

27. As Ronald Goldman has pointed out with regard to the use of biblical material with children in *Religious Thinking from Childhood to Adolescence* (London: Routledge and Kegan Paul, 1964).

28. By pointing to such conflicts as central to religious experience and language, I do not mean to suggest that one can simply mechanically go through the Bible looking for where such questions are dealt with, discarding the rest as not religiously relevant. Such issues are seldom confronted baldly; rather, they are encountered through other conflicts and everyday experiences when for various reasons one's reality suddenly finds itself backed into a corner, when in asking a controlled informational question of "What must I do to be saved?" the reply "Go, sell all . . . " comes back. Suddenly, it's not more of the same, but a challenge to one's whole conception of himself and his world.

chapter 4 religious experience and language in the old testament

1. Arthur Koestler describes conflict as essential to any dramatic novel; see *The Act of Creation* (New York: Dell, 1964), chap. 19, especially pp. 350ff.

2. See Claude Lévi-Strauss, *Structural Anthropology* (Garden City, N.Y.: Doubleday, 1963), trans. C. Jacobson and B.G. Schoepf.

3. See Klaus Baltzer, "Naboth's Weinberg," *Wort und Dienst* 8 (1965): 73-88. This conflict is intrinsic to the situation where nomadic and nonnomadic society meet. The Mari texts from the first half of the second millenium reflect the relations of this city on the middle Euphrates River with surrounding seminomadic tribes in different stages of transition toward settled life. Cf. A. Malamat, "Mari," *Biblical Archaeologist* 34 (1971), especially p. 19. Legal circumventions were used to avoid the prohibition on nontransfer of land.

4. Systems is used as set forth by Talcott Parsons in *Societies: Evolutionary and Comparative Perspectives* (Englewood Cliffs, N.J.: Prentice-Hall, 1966), pp. 1-29. The four basic systems are (1) behavioral organism, (2) personality system, (3) social system, and (4) cultural system.

5. See Barnabas Lindars, "Ezekiel and Individual Responsibility," *Vetus Testamentum* XV (1965): 452-67.

6. Cf. Koestler, *Act of Creation,* p. 347: "Such perceptual codes function as selective filters, as it were; the filter rejects as 'wrong' anything which does not fit its 'mesh'; and accepts or 'recognizes' anything that fits it, i.e., which gives the same 'general impression.'"

7. Isaiah 6; Jeremiah 1; Ezekiel 2—3; and compare Jeremiah 4:10, where it is said that Yahweh has deceived the people with the "lying spirit" sent by Yahweh in the vision of Micaiah ben Imlah in 1 Kings 22.

8. *Structural Anthropology,* p. 199. Used by permission. Lévi-Strauss comments, "Form defines itself by opposition to a content which is exterior to it; but structure has no content: it is itself the content, apprehended in a logical organization conceived as a property of the real" (quoted by Peter Caws in "What Is Structuralism?," reprinted from *Partisan Review* XXXV:1 [Winter 1968]: 75-91, in E.N. and Tanya Hayes, eds., *Claude Lévi-Strauss: The Anthropologist as Hero* [Cambridge, Mass.: M.I.T. Press, 1970], p. 203). For a survey of the form (rhetoric)-content question with special attention to the linguistic perspective, see Karl D. Utti, *Linguistics and Literary Theory* (Englewood Cliffs, N.J.: Prentice-Hall, 1969).

9. Whallon, *Formula, Character, and Context: Studies in Homeric, Old English, and Old Testament Poetry* (Washington, D.C.: Center for Hellenic Studies, 1969).

10. The reader is alerted for something unusual by the use of the "Word of God" formula in verse 9 which normally stands directly before an oracle. In this case the oracle comes only after the "exhaustion" stage of the intervening theophany in verses 15-18.

11. Roland Barthes, "Historical Discourse," reprinted from *Social Science Information* VI:4 (August 1967), in *Introduction to Structuralism,* ed. Michael Lane (New York: Basic Books, 1970), p. 152. His other two types are the metaphorical form (lyrical and symbolic) and the metonymic form (epic).

12. The oracle leaves the audience to write its own conclusion. For remarks on narrative trends in this same direction, see Umberto Eco, *L'OEuvre ouverte* (Paris: 1965). A sympathetic review of Eco's book is in G. de Mallac's "The Poetics of the Open Form," *Books Abroad* 45 (Winter 1971): 31-36.

13. Cf. Warren Weaver's comments on probability and choice in "The Mathematics of Communication," reprinted from pp. 11-15 of *Scientific American* (July 1949), in *Science and Literature: New Lenses for Criticism,* ed. Edward M.

Jennings (Garden City, N.Y.: Doubleday, 1970), p. 19; also the comment of Jennings on p. 14. The genre used in 2 Samuel 12 and 1 Kings 14 has been form-critically analyzed as a juridical parable by Ulrich Simon, "The Poor Man's Ewe-Lamb: An Example of a Juridical Parable," *Biblica* 48 (1967): 207-42. But the self-conviction device is much more extensive than any one genre and is one obvious way in which a person may be brought to the point of readiness to experience a perceptual shift.

14. On the significance of context, see Weaver, "Mathematics of Communication," p. 27.

15. See my article "The Righteousness of Noah," *Vetus Testamentum* XXI (1971): 261-80.

16. The model used by Thomas S. Kuhn in his *The Structure of Scientific Revolutions* (Chicago: University of Chicago Press, 1970) of a shift from one common paradigm to another, suggested by David H. Fischer in *Historians' Fallacies: Toward a Logic of Historical Thought* (New York: Harper & Row, 1970), pp. 161-62, as a generally applicable alternative to the "genesis" perspective on history, seems to be applicable to the study of the perceptual shift as reflected in literature.

17. E.g., the image of a plague in Jeremiah 4:5-8, 13-22; see Georg Fohrer (-E. Sellin)'s *Introduction to the Old Testament* (Nashville, Tenn.: Abingdon Press, 1968), pp. 349-50. Luis Alonso-Schökel speaks of the image as a first form of the formless experience, a linguistic image, in "Stilistiche Analyse," *Supplements to Vetus Testamentum* VII (1960): 159.

18. C.S. Lewis comments, "Only that which to some degree enlightens ourselves is likely to enlighten others," *Science and Literature,* p. 60, a reprint of "Bluspels and Flalansferes: A Semantic Nightmare" from *Rehabilitations and Other Essays* (Folcroft, Pa.: Folcroft Press).

19. Excerpted from Chapter 10, "The Effectiveness of Symbols," p. 197 (originally published under the title "L'Efficacité symbolique," in Revue de l'Historie des Religions, CXXXV, No. 1, 1949, pp. 5-27) in *Structural Anthropology* by Claude Levi-Strauss, translated by Brooke Grundfest Schoepf, © 1963 by Basic Books, Inc., Publishers, New York. "The effectiveness of symbols would consist precisely in this 'inductive property' by which formally homologous structures, built out of different materials at different levels of life—organic processes, unconscious mind, rational thought—are related to one another" (ibid.). A parallel point is made by Merleau-Ponty in *Signs.*

20. Cf. William Empson, *Seven Types of Ambiguity* (New York: New Directions, 1947), and *The Structure of Complex Words* (Ann Arbor, Mich.: University of Michigan Press, 1951).

21. See my article, "A Legal Background to the Yahwist's Use of 'Good and Evil' in Genesis 2-3," *Journal of Biblical Literature* 88 (1969): 277-78.

22. *Concepts of Criticism,* ed. Stephen G. Nichols, Jr. (New Haven, Conn.: Yale University Press, 1963), p. 353.

23. The text must be seen as a unity; cf. James Muilenburg, "The Intercession of the Covenant Mediator," in *Words and Meanings,* ed. Peter R. Ackroyd and Barnabas Lindars (Cambridge: Cambridge University Press, 1968), pp. 159-81. On insight and nondiscursive knowledge, see Susanne K. Langer, *Philosophy in a New Key: A Study in The Symbolism of Reason, Rite and Art* (New York: New American Library, 1951), especially pp. 172-73, 190-91, 246-47.

24. R.B.Y. Scott, "The Literary Structure of Isaiah's Oracles," in *Studies in Old Testament Prophecy Presented to Professor Theodore H. Robinson,* ed. Harold H. Rowley (Edinburgh: T. & T. Clark, 1950), pp. 175-86.

25. Brevard Childs, *Isaiah and the Assyrian Crisis,* Studies in Biblical Theology, Second Series, No. 3 (London: SCM Press, 1967).

26. Klaus Koch, *The Growth of the Biblical Tradition: The Form-Critical Method,* trans. S.M. Cupitt (New York: Charles Scribner's Sons, 1969), pp. 193-94.

27. Georg Fohrer, "Jesaja I als Zusammenfassung der Verkündigung Jesajas," *Zeitschrift für die alttestamentliche Wissenschaft* 74 (1962): 251-68; Walther Zimmerli *(Ezechiel,* Biblischer Kommentar Altes Testament XIII [Neukirchen-Vluyn: Neukirchener Verlag, 1959-69]); Claus Westermann, *Isaiah 40—66,* The Old Testament Library, trans. David M. Stalker (Philadelphia: Westminster Press, 1969).

28. Otto Eissfeldt's giving priority to the short oracle may be correct for the general historical development, but this process cannot be transferred to the production of each prophetic oracle; see his *The Old Testament: An Introduction,* trans. Peter R. Ackroyd (New York: Harper & Row, 1965), p. 79.

29. Robin W. Winks, *The Historian as Detective: Essays on Evidence* (New York: Harper & Row, 1968), p. xxi.

30. Peter Berger, *A Rumor of Angels: Modern Sociology and the Rediscovery of the Supernatural* (New York: Doubleday, 1969), p. 72.

31. Gerhard von Rad, "Faith Reckoned as Righteousness," in *The Problem of the Hexateuch and Other Essays,* trans. E.W.T. Dicken (New York: McGraw-Hill, 1966), pp. 125-30. The verb *'mn* normally takes neither an "in" clause (to believe in) nor an impersonal accusative (to believe "something"). Cf. H. Wildberger, *Jesaja,* Biblischer Kommentar Altes Testament XI (Neukirchen-Vluyn: Neukirchener Verlag, 1965ff.), p. 285, regarding the change by the Chronicler who does use an "in" clause.

32. See my "The Righteousness of Noah" where the reference to Müller is given.

33. Jean L'Hour, *Die Ethik der Bundestradition im Alten Testament,* Stuttgarter Bibelstudien 14 (Stuttgart: Verlag Katholisches Bibelwerk, 1967), trans. M. Breithaupt from French.

34. Eugene Nida and Charles Taber, *The Theory and Practice of Translation* (Leiden: E.J. Brill, 1969), p. 24. Used by permission.

35. Donald C. Freeman, ed., *Linguistics and Literary Style* (New York: Holt, Rinehart & Winston, 1970).

36. This assumes that the meaning of a word is not only or necessarily primarily a *thing* to which it refers. For examples of further discussion, see (a) by a linguist: John Lyons, *Introduction to Theoretical Linguistics* (Cambridge: Cambridge University Press, 1968), pp. 404-81; (b) by a literary critic: C.K. Ogden and I.A. Richards, *The Meaning of Meaning: A Study of the Influence of Language Upon Thought and of the Science of Symbolism* (New York: Harcourt, Brace & World, 1923); (c) by a philosopher: Willard Van O. Quine, *Word and Object* (Cambridge, Mass.: M.I.T. Press, 1960).

37. For example: Roman Jakobson, a linguist with strong interests in the study of literature and a continental background (where the separation between linguistics and literary criticism was never so sharp as in America), outlines six functions: (1) referential (basically the "information," what is denoted); (2) emotive (relating to the expression of the addresser); (3) conative (what is evoked from the addressee—conative roughly corresponds to the commonly used connotative); (4) phatic (to maintain contact between the addresser and addressee as in a greeting); (5) metalingual (conversation about the message: "Did you mean this?"); and (6) poetic (parallelism, etc.). See Jakobson, "Closing Statement: Linguistics and Poetics," in *Style in Language,* ed. Thomas A. Sebeok (Cambridge, Mass.: M.I.T. Press, 1960), pp. 350-77, especially pp. 353-59. Although biblical scholars have naturally practiced literary criticism, they have not been greatly affected by general

developments in the field of literary criticism. Two exceptions have unfortunately written their major works in languages which make them inaccessible to many biblical scholars: Luis Alonso-Schökel, *Estudios de Poética Hebrea* (Barcelona: Imprenta Claraso, 1963), in Spanish; and M. Weiss, *The Bible and Modern Literary Theory*, 2d ed. (Jerusalem: 1967), in modern Hebrew. The lively discussion of the relation of linguistics and literary criticism over the past decade has had no noticeable effect on biblical studies.

38. Their results (for a particular test) if not contradictory (which they often seem to be) at least present problems of integration into a comprehensive interpretation. A linguistic approach extends the structural approach to the syntax of a sentence to larger units of discourse. Stylistics tends to study the author's own creative role in forming his material. Form criticism focuses on the genre of the text and the social (rather than individual) setting out of which the genre arises. The parallel to Talcott Parsons' four basic systems of society is suggestive. We recall that these systems (with my suggested parallels) are the organism (language), personality (stylistics), social (form criticism), and cultural ("meaning"). Parsons' model (1) provides a theoretical context for the different approaches to the study of the text and explicitly relates them to levels of expression of the text; (2) helps define the borders between the approaches and their rationale; (3) helps deal with the relationship between the approaches, including both (a) their relative position in a hierarchy of significance and (b) their intermixture (e.g., the manifestation in the societal system of cultural, societal, personality, and organism components).

39. Nida and Taber, *Translation*, p. 4.

40. Amos Wilder, *The New Voice: Religion, Literature, Hermeneutics* (New York: Herder & Herder, 1969), pp. 67-68.

41. Hans Schmid, *Gerechtigkeit als Weltordnung: Hintergrund und Geschichte des alttestamentlichen Gerechtigkeitsbegriffes*, Beitrage zur Historischen Theologie 40 (Tübingen: J.C.B. Mohr, 1968), pp. 4-7.

42. Geo Widengren, *Religionsphänomenologie*, trans. R. Elgnowski from Swedish (Berlin: W. de Gruyter, 1969).

43. James Barr, "The Symbolism of Names in the Old Testament," *Bulletin of the John Rylands Library* 52 (1969): 11-29.

44. William F. Albright, *New Horizons in Biblical Research* (London: Oxford University Press, 1966), p. 30.

45. Burke Long, *The Problem of Etiological Narrative in the Old Testament*, Beihefte zur Zeitschrift für die alttestamentliche Wissenschaft 108 (Berlin: Verlag A. Töpelmann, 1968).

46. Max Black, *The Labyrinth of Language* (New York: New American Library, 1969), pp. 108, 203, 207.

47. Wilder, *New Voice*, p. 150. Used by permission.

48. See J. Holladay, Jr., "The Day(s) the Moon Stood Still," *Journal of Biblical Literature* 87 (1968): 166-78.

49. Wilder, *New Voice*, p. 105.

50. Barthes, "Historical Discourse," pp. 152ff.

51. Wilder, *New Voice*, pp. 115-19.

52. W. Sibley Towner, "On Calling People 'Prophets' in 1970," *Interpretation* 24 (1970): 492-509.

53. Mary Douglas (summarizing the position of Lévi-Strauss), "The Meaning of Myth," in Edmund R. Leach, ed., *The Structural Study of Myth and Totemism* (London: Tavistock, 1967), p. 57.

54. Lévi-Strauss calls myth "the most fundamental form of inauthenticity" in

George Charbonnier, *Conversations with Claude Lévi-Strauss,* trans. J. and D. Weightman (London: Jonathan Cape, 1969; published in America by Grossman Publishers, Inc.), p. 55. On the correspondence of myth and literature cf. Peter Caws in Hayes and Hayes, eds., *Lévi-Strauss,* p. 202.

chapter 5 debunking and the open society

1. Peter Berger and Thomas Luckmann, *The Social Construction of Reality: A Treatise in the Sociology of Knowledge* (Garden City, N.Y.: Doubleday, 1966).

2. Peter Berger and Stanley Pullberg, "Reification and the Sociological Critique of Consciousness," *New Left Review* 35 (1966): 56-71; of older works see especially Karl Mannheim, *Ideology and Utopia: An Introduction to the Sociology of Knowledge* (New York: Harcourt, Brace & World, 1936), who on p. 64 speaks of a debunking tendency which is directed against the ideological element in man's thinking.

3. In "The Meaning of 'Mythology' in Relation to the Old Testament," *Vetus Testamentum* 9 (1959): 1-10, Barr emphasizes three aspects of correspondence: (1) between the then and now, (2) between heaven and earth, and (3) between god and man.

4. Cf. the statement of David Maybury-Lewis in summarizing the position of Lévi-Strauss ("Science by Association," p. 136 in *Claude Lévi-Strauss; The Anthropologist as Hero,* ed. E.N. and Tanya Hayes [Cambridge, Mass.: M.I.T. Press, 1970], reprinted from *The Hudson Review* 20:4 [Winter 1967-68]: 707-11): "Myths do not try to explain natural phenomena but rather use natural phenomena as a medium of explanation, as they try to resolve the contradictions with which man is inevitably faced." For a sympathetic and not overly complicated discussion of Lévi-Strauss, see Edmund R. Leach, *Claude Lévi-Strauss* (New York: Viking, 1970). On the abstractness of myth, see Peter Caws, "What Is Structuralism?," in Hayes and Hayes, eds., *Lévi-Strauss,* pp. 75-91.

5. This explains in part the a-metaphysical orientation of the Old Testament and its language.

6. See William F. Albright, "Samuel and the Beginnings of the Prophetic Movement," in *Interpreting the Prophetic Tradition,* ed. Harry M. Orlinsky (New York: KTAV, 1969), pp. 149-76.

7. George Coates, *The Murmuring Motif in the Wilderness Traditions of the Old Testament* (Nashville, Tenn.: Abingdon Press, 1968).

8. See the discussion in chapter 4 and in my "The Righteousness of Noah," *Vetus Testamentum* XXI (1971): 261-80.

9. Walther Zimmerli, *Ezechiel,* Biblischer Kommentar Altes Testament XIII (Neukirchen-Vluyn: Neukirchener Verlag, 1959-69). Cf. Amos Wilder's remarks on the New Testament's and Jesus' reappropriation of language in *The New Voice: Religion, Literature, Hermeneutics* (New York: Herder & Herder, 1969), pp. 109, 112-13. For the primacy of the image over the myth, see Beatrice Goff, *Symbols of Prehistoric Mesopotamia* (New Haven, Conn.: Yale University Press, 1963).

10. How could the prophet do this? Albright speaks of a kind of empirico-logic which he distinguishes both from primitive mentality and from Greek "postulational reasoning." This he links particularly with the prophets. So far as this empirical logic is intrinsically linked up with a closeness to experience, it may correlate with the debunking role of Old Testament prophets. Cf. Albright, "Samuel," pp. 151ff., and "The Ancient Israelite Mind in Its Environmental Context," chap. 2 of *New Horizons in Biblical Research,* pp. 17-35. Note also Peter Berger's comment on "Protestantism, the first religious tradition that found the

courage to turn the sharp instruments of empirical inquiry back upon itself" in *A Rumor of Angels: Modern Society and the Rediscovery of the Supernatural* (New York: Doubleday, 1969), p. 84.

11. Berger and Pullberg, "Reification," pp. 69-70.

12. Obviously the antecedent stages are important, including the patriarchal input with its concepts of a people on the way and a nonspacebound god. But we must not assume that the seminomadic patriarchal clans were any less mythological than their counterparts in the settled lands.

13. Eric D. Hirsch, Jr., in discussing hypotheses which generate their own data, points to the self-confirmability of all interpretation. This is normally what happens also in terms of "world views." Even the presence and knowledge of an alternative is not necessarily relativizing so long as one operates from within an intact system. But what happens when the alternatives are present, the system is no longer intact, and one is only marginally within the system? This was the situation of Israel at the time of its consolidation. See his *Validity in Interpretation* (New Haven, Conn.: Yale University Press, 1967), pp. 166ff.

14. To what extent this could be argued for other prophets (and Jesus from Galilee) requires further investigation. Note McClelland's and Hagen's emphasis on the social marginality of the entrepreneur-type individual and group as an agent for change (Richard P. Appelbaum, *Theories of Social Change* [Chicago: Markham, 1970], pp. 125-26. The role of charisma in Israel was first emphasized by Max Weber and has been linked by Albright ("Samuel," p. 167) with the self-criticism which is central to our present concern.

15. Narrative was more immediately suitable than oracle because of the continuity between narrative and myth; see Roland Barthes, "Historical Discourse," in M. Lane, ed., *Introduction to Structuralism* (New York: Basic Books, 1970), p. 155.

16. Lévi-Strauss comments: "We should not, then, draw a distinction between 'societies with no history' and 'societies which have histories.' In fact, every human society has a history. . . . But whereas so-called primitive societies are surrounded by the substance of history and try to remain impervious to it, modern societies interiorize history, as it were, and turn it into the motive power of their development" (quoted in George Charbonnier, *Conversations with Claude Lévi-Strauss*, trans. J. and D. Weightman [London: Jonathan Cape, 1969; published in America by Grossman Publishers, Inc.], p. 39). Maybury-Lewis ("Science by Association," in Hayes and Hayes, eds., *Lévi-Strauss*, p. 137) notes, "Totemic societies explain themselves in terms of a *Weltanschauung* [world view] that incorporates changes into itself while remaining ostensibly immutable. They are in sharp contrast to societies that admit the notion of flux as part of their self-image and therefore explain themselves by history."

17. Charbonnier, *Conversations,* p. 33.

18. Marc Gaboriau, "Structural Anthropology and History," in Michael Lane, ed., *Structuralism,* p. 163, reprinted from *L'Esprit* 322 (1963).

19. Barthes, *Structuralism,* p. 153 distinguishes two categories of meaning, in historical discourse, implicit and superimposed meaning. In the Old Testament these are exemplified respectively by the accession narrative (2 Samuel 9—1 Kings 2) and the Deuteronomistic history.

20. See Edwin Muir, *The Structure of the Novel* (New York: Harcourt, Brace & World, n.d.), for relevant comments on epic, chronicle, and novel. For views of history, see the essays in *The Idea of History in the Ancient Near East,* ed. Robert C. Dentan (New Haven, Conn.: Yale University Press, 1955). For examples of the

various types of texts mentioned, see James B. Pritchard, ed., *Ancient Near Eastern Texts Relating to the Old Testament*, rev. ed. (Princeton, N.J.: Princeton University Press, 1969).

21. See George Steiner, "Orpheus with His Myths," in Hayes and Hayes, *Lévi-Strauss*, p. 176. David Fischer, *Historians' Fallacies: Toward a Logic of Historical Thought* (New York: Harper & Row, 1970), p. 132, notes that the child locates all figures of the American past on a single chronological plane. On p. 147 Fischer discusses the problem of when "the historical revolution, i.e., the moment of a great expansion in historical consciousness," took place. Correctly he says that this is an illegitimate question. It objectifies a process. While the two pure types of society do not exist, yet the distinction in terms of whether one looks to experience as a realm of meaning seems valid when contrasted with a reified world view of mythology.

22. Cf. J. Gwyn Griffiths, *The Conflict of Honus and Seth* (Liverpool: Liverpool University Press, 1960); Bertil Albrektson, *History and the Gods: An Essay on the Idea of Historical Events as Divine Manifestations in the Ancient Near East and in Israel* (Lund, Sweden: CWK Gleerup, 1967).

23. Myth looks at the world synchronically (a-historically). Cf. Peter Caws's comment (in Hayes and Hayes, *Lévi-Strauss*, p. 203): "To say that the world is intelligible means that it presents itself to the mind of the primitive as a message, to which his language and behavior are an appropriate response—but not as a message from elsewhere, simply as a message, as it were, in its own right." The terms diachronic (as in historical grammar) and synchronic (as in descriptive grammar which ignores historical antecedents) offer a better contrast than do historical and a-historical.

24. Eberhard Otto, "Geschichtsbild und Geschichtsschreibung in "Agypten," *Welt des Orient* 3 (1966): 161-76. Berger and Pullberg, "Reification," pp. 67ff., discuss the reifications of roles in which man expresses roles rather than a role being man's expression of himself. Man's experience is subordinated to and receives its significance only as it repeats prototypical action.

25. Hayes and Hayes, eds., *Lévi-Strauss*, p. 137.

26. Erich Auerbach, *Mimesis: The Representation of Reality in Western Literature*, trans. Willard R. Trask (Princeton, N.J.: Princeton University Press, 1953), pp. 1-93.

27. Adda Bozeman, *The Future of Law in a Multicultural World* (Princeton, N.J.: Princeton University Press, 1971).

28. Cf. the discussion by Langdon Gilkey, *Naming the Whirlwind: The Renewal of God-Language* (Indianapolis, Ind.: Bobbs-Merrill, 1969), pp. 31-73.

29. See Horst Preuss, *Jahwehglaube und Zukunftserwartung* (Stuttgart: W. Kohlhammer, 1968), especially pp. 154-214. For Preuss, eschatology is not something added to an earlier core: "Yahweh faith is future expectation." His understanding is similar to that of Wolfhart Pannenberg.

30. See Hans-Peter Müller, *Ursprünge and Strukturen alttestamentliche Eschatologie*, Beihefte zur Zeitschrift für die alttestamentliche Wissenschaft 109 (Berlin: Verlag A. Töpelmann, 1969). According to Müller the two factors giving rise to the aporia (contradiction) are: (1) certain interventions of God in history were experienced as possessed of an ultimate validity and finality; (2) subsequent developments always proved the relativity of each divine intervention. Müller's interpretation has certain similarities to the position of Jurgen Moltmann.

31. Müller's thesis concerning the aporia is in many ways similar to the debunking thrust but is seen from a different perspective and given an almost diametrically opposed implicit valuation.

32. Preuss's critique that older historical explanations are inadequate because the same conditions occurred elsewhere is first inaccurate and second an example of the fallacy of the general law of universal hypothesis in which "an explanation is not complete unless 'it might as well have functioned as a prediction'" (David Fischer, *Historians' Fallacies,* p. 128, quoting Carl Hempel). Also implicit in Preuss is a misleading understanding of patriarchal religion as basically historical and nonmythological. This can be maintained only by playing loose with the various meanings of history. Further, there is no reason to assume that Israel's patriarchal religion was basically different in this regard from that of other Semitic peoples in a similar sociohistorical context (e.g., earlier at Mari and later among the Nabateans).

33. Preuss's rejection of previous historical answers is also wrong because his comparison is atomistic. My suggestion is that the reason why eschatology did not develop elsewhere in the ancient Near East is because there myth already fulfilled the role which gave rise to eschatology in Israel.

34. For some other aspects of the authority questions, see chapters 1 and 6. A closely related question is that of the validity of one's interpretation. For a significant discussion which runs counter to that of the New Hermeneutics, see Erik D. Hirsch, Jr., *Validity in Interpretation.*

35. Auerbach, *Mimesis,* p. 15.

36. In *Before Philosophy: The Intellectual Adventure of Ancient Man* (Baltimore, Md.: Penguin Books, 1959), pp. 244-45.

37. Talcott Parsons, *Societies: Evolutionary and Comparative Perspectives* (Englewood Cliffs, N.J.: Prentice-Hall, 1966), pp. 98ff.

38. Gregory Bateson and Jurgen Ruesch, *Communication: The Social Matrix of Psychiatry* (New York: W.W. Norton & Co., 1968), pp. 176, 181.

39. René Wellek and Austin Warren, *Theory of Literature,* 3d ed. (New York: Harcourt, Brace & World, 1963), pp. 152, 156.

40. Wilder, *New Voice,* p. 106. Used by permission.

41. Peter Berger, "Charisma and Religious Innovation: The Social Structure of Israelite Prophecy," *American Sociological Review* 28 (1963): 940-50.

42. Wellek and Warren, *Theory of Literature,* p. 151.

43. Wilder, *New Voice,* p. 117.

44. Edwin Muir, *Structure of the Novel,* p. 60.

45. Ibid., pp. 91 and 63 (italics added).

46. Parsons, *Societies,* pp. 101-2.

47. See Johann J. Stamm and Maurice E. Andrew, *The Ten Commandments in Recent Research,* Studies in Biblical Theology, second series 2 (London: SCM Press, 1967), p. 104.

48. Cf. Hans Schmid, *Gerechtigkeit als Weltordnung: Hintergrund und Geschichte des alttestamentlichen Gerechtigkeitsbegriffes* (Tübingen: J.C.B. Mohr, 1968), pp. 46-66.

49. Walter Eisenbeis, *Die Wurzel* שׁלם *im Alten Testament,* Beihefte zur Zeitschrift für die alttestamentliche Wissenschaft 113 (Berlin: W. de Gruyter, 1969), pp. 166, 355.

50. Wellek and Warren, *Theory of Literature,* p. 153.

51. Ibid., pp. 154, 156.

52. Cf. Hugo G. Nutini, "Some Considerations on the Nature of Social Structure and Model Building: A Critique of Claude Lévi-Strauss and Edmund Leach," reprinted from *American Anthropologist* 67 (1965): 707-31, in Hayes and Hayes, eds., *Lévi-Strauss,* pp. 100-6.

53. Erhard Gerstenberger, *Wesen und Herkunft des "Apodiktischen Rechts,"*

Wissenschaftliche Monographien zum Alten und Neuen Testament 20 (Neu-kirchen-Vluyn: Neukirchener Verlag, 1965). Gerstenberger further does not think that apodictic law is technically to be classified as law.

54. Norbert Lohfink, "Zur Dekalogfassung von Dt 5," *Biblische Zeitschrift* NF 9 (1965): 17-32.

55. Berend Gemser, *Supplements to Vetus Testamentum* I, pp. 50-66.

56. Jean Piaget *(Structuralism,* trans. C. Maschler [New York: Basic Books, 1970], p. 5) notes three key ideas of structuralism: (1) wholeness; (2) transformation; (3) self-regulation. "Constructionism" (cf. below) is related to self-regulation. A more "neutral" introduction is provided by Michael Lane *(Introduction to Structural-ism,* pp. 11-34): (1) the "code" or language as the object of analysis; (2) focus of attention on the structure rather than on the individual elements; (3) basic structures exist beneath the surface; (4) concept of innatism which limits the possible ways of structuring by man (contrast Piaget here); (5) emphasis on binary opposition; (6) focus on synchronic structures and laws of transformation rather than on "cause and effect."

57. Lévi-Strauss comments that "conscious models, which are usually known as 'norms,' are by definition very poor ones, since they are not intended to explain the phenomena but to perpetuate them" (excerpted from Chapter 14, "The Serpent with Fish inside His Body," p. 273 [originally published under the title "Le Serpent au corps rempli de poissons," in Actes du XXVIIIe Congrès des Am-éricanistes (Paris: 1947; Société des Américanistes, 1948), pp. 633-36] in *(Structural Anthropology* by Claude Lévi-Strauss, translated by Brooke Gundfest Schoepf, © 1963 by Basic Books, Inc., Publishers, New York). CF. also Piaget, *Structuralism,* p. 108.

58. Cf. Piaget, *Structuralism,* p. 35: "There *is* no 'form as such' or 'content as such,' . . . each element . . . is always simultaneously form to the content it subsumes and content for some higher form." Cf. also p. 29.

59. Cf. Piaget's discussion (pp. 105-6) of Hans Kelsen's conception of the juridical structure as a pyramid of norms at whose peak is the "fundamental norm" which is the source of legitimacy of the whole pyramid. But the fundamental norm remains to be accounted for, and at this point we must move from surface to deep structure.

60. The intermediate stages in the development of the term Torah include application to individual law, expansion to include a particular corpus and then implicitly the whole of the law given by God, and finally the Pentateuch in which that law was contained. It begins as directed to individual experience and ends up being applied to the experience of the people as a whole. In his recent study *(Gestalt und Bezeichnung alttestamentlicher Rechtssätze. Eine formgeschicht-lich-terminologische Studie,* Wissenschaftliche Monographien zum Alten und Neuen Testament 39 [Neukirchen-Vluyn: Neukirchener Verlag, 1971]), Gerhard Liedke pushes the usage of Torah back one stage further when he suggests a profane usage (as in wisdom instructions) being prior to the specialized priestly usage.

61. Piaget, *Structuralism,* p. 34.

62. Basically this amounts to the form-content hierarchy being transferred to the deep level. Piaget comments: "The idea of *structure* as a system of transforma-tions becomes continuous with that of *construction* as continual formation" *(Structuralism,* p. 34; see also pp. 60-68, 90-91, and 102ff.).

63. In order not to complicate further a difficult subject, I have worked with the basic surface level–deep level model. Some suggest this model may need further refinement, including at least a third level which mediates between the first two.

Such a third level might be related to some of the phenomena discussed in this paragraph which seem to exercise "control" long before they become explicit.

64. Marc Gaboriau, in Lane, ed., *Structuralism*, p.163, emphasizes that the basis of change lies in a lack of harmony between the various systems. The same point is made by Parsons (in *Societies)* and other sociologists; cf. Appelbaum, *Theories of Social Change*, p. 43.

chapter 6   experienced jesus and christ event

1. From *Biblical Theology in Crisis*, by Brevard S. Childs, p. 119, italics added. Copyright ©MCMLXX, The Westminster Press. Used by permission.

2. See George Kretschmar, *Studien zur fruhchristlichen Trinitätstheologie* (Tübingen: J.C.B. Mohr, 1956).

3. See Krister Stendahl, "The Apostle Paul and the Introspective Conscience of the West," *Harvard Theological Review*, 1963, pp. 199-215.